monday morning

HOW TO MAKE

CRAFTS FROM TRASH

Easy-to-Make Crafts from Recyclable Materials

by Marilynn G. Barr

Contents

Introduction 6
  Reuseable Materials List 7
  Environmental Issues 8
  Things to Do to Make a Difference.....9
  Eco-News 10

Arts and Crafts Tools
  Styrofoam Stencils......................11
  Baby Food Jar Supply Storage 12
  Coffee Can Crayon Box 13
  Plastic Lid Stencils and Templates 14
  Dry Pen Scratching Tool 15
  Yarn and Cardboard Portfolio 16
  Hand Towel Paintbrush Wallet...........17
  Glitter Dispenser......................18
  Mustard Bottle Paint Dispensers 19
  Sponge Stamps......................20
  Old Plate Palette 21
  Twist Tie Needles 22
  Plastic Lid Texture Tools 23
  Cardboard Weaving Loom 24
  Jar Lid Pin Cushion 25

Bird Feeders
  Soda Bottle Feeder 26
  Straw Hat Feeder 27
  Margarine Tub Feeder 28
  Oatmeal Container Bird Feeder 29
  Egg Carton Feeder 30
  Flower Pot Feeder 31

Costumes
  Tiger
  Stryrofoam Tiger Mask......................32
  Tiger Stripes T-shirt 33
  Tiger Stripe Socks 34
  Fish
  Styrofoam Fish Mask 35
  Plastic Lid Fish Scale T-shirt............36
  Bird
  Styrofoam Bird Mask 37
  Feather T-shirt 38
  Elephant
  Styrofoam Elephant Mask......................39
  Grocery Bag Elephant Vest 40
  Elephant Toe Socks 41
  Space Creature
  Space Creature Mask 42
  Bubble Wrap Vest 43
  Alien Sock Feet 44

  Knight
  Milk Container Helmet 45
  Pillow Case Knight 's Tunic......................46
  Knight Boots 47

Decorations
  Plastic Milk Container Butterflies 48
  Plastic Grocery Bag Bunnies 49
  Bottle Character 50
  Jar Lid Wind Chimes 51
  Egg Carton Flowers 52
  Detergent Bottle Sculpture 53
  Terra Cotta Flower Pot People 54
  Pie Tin Punch Ornament 55
  Plastic Lid Refrigerator Magnet........56
  Resealable Bag Sun Catcher 57
  Broken Flower Pot Nature Collage 58
  Artificial Flower Collage 59
  Old Clothing Appliques 60
  Plastic Collar Critter 61
  Plastic Hair Ornament 62

Displays
  Drink Can Holder Collage 63
  Cereal Box Village......................64
  Broken Tile Mosaic 65
  Woven Necktie Wall Hanging 66
  Checkbook Box Collector's Display....67
  Berry Basket Dry Flower Display 68
  Scrap Wire Sculpture 69
  Crushed Eggshell Painting 70
  Artificial Flowers Window Display.....71
  Paper Towel Tube 3-D Collage 72
  Packing Peanuts Sculpture 73
  Tissue and Oatmeal Box Robot 74
  Tissue Boxcars 75
  Clothing Label Collage 76
  Styrofoam Tray Scrimshaw 77
  Molded Drink-Holder 3-D Painting....78

Garden Tools and Yard Art
  Plastic Lid Bumble Bees 79
  Potting Soil Scoops 80
  Paint Stirrer Plant Stakes 81
  Egg Carton Seed Planters 82
  Soda Bottle Bird Seed Scoops..........83
  Wind Wigglers 84
  Paint Can Tool Carrier 85
  Cream Cheese Planter 86

Gifts

Bottle Cap Checkers 87
Coffee Can Lid Fan 88
Craft Tissue Juice Jar Vases 89
Artsy Soap Dispenser 90
Wallpaper Keepsake Boxes 91
Greeting Card Scrapbook 92
Memory Stones in a Jar 93
Paper Towel Tube Napkin Rings 94
Yarn-Wrapped Picture Frame 95
Compact Disk Case Picture Frames ... 96
Cutoff Blue Jeans Tote Bag 97
Blue Jean Books 98
Newspaper Gift Wrap 99
Mitten Sachet 100
Paint Can Game Tote 101
Egg Carton Jewelry Box 102
Poster Board Memory Quilt 103
Painted Walking Stick 104
Plastic Milk Bottle Bookmarks 105
Ribbon Clad Flower Pot 106

Holidays

Canada Day
Canada Day Flower Pot 107
Maple Leaf Sponge Stencilling 108

Chinese New Year
Egg Carton Dragon 109
Plastic Lid Animal Coasters 110

Christmas
Styrofoam Tray Christmas Tree 111
Old Compact Disk Tree Ornaments . 112
Plastic Snowman Bookmarks 113

Cinco de Mayo
Cinco de Mayo Display Plate 114
Styrofoam Tray Lacing Cards 115

Diwali
Glass Jar Dipa Lamps 116
Aluminum Pie Tin Dipa Lamps 117

Easter
Sawdust and Glue Egg Basket 118
Plastic Milk Bottle Bunny 119
Grocery Bag Bunny Basket 120
Woven Berry Basket 121
Jelly Bean Dispenser 122

Father's Day
Paper Towel Tube Tie Rack 123
Plastic Lid Sock Matchers 124

Hanukkah
Dinner Plate Menorah 125
Paper Cup Menorah 126
Plastic Lid Menorah Display 127

Halloween
Styrofoam Tray Pumpkin Garland ... 128
Milk Container Jack-o'-lantern 129
Jar Lid Pumpkin Checkers 130

Independence Day
Stars and Stripes Sleeve Hats 131
Stars and Stripes Lid Badge 132

Kwanzaa
Egg Carton Kinara 133
Old Baseball Cap Holiday Hat 134

Mardi Gras
Mardi Gras Button Necklaces 135
Paper Bead Necklaces 136
Tray and Egg Carton Masks 137

Mother's Day
Mom's Keys Margarine Lid 138
Greeting Card Flower Bouquet 139
Flower Wreath 140

St. Patrick's Day
ShamRocks 141
Paper Cup Leprechauns 142
Bottle Cap Gold Coins 143

Thanksgiving
Grocery Bag Cornucopia Collage 144
Old Baseball Cap Turkey 145
Ten Little Turkeys Glove Puppets ... 146

Valentine's Day
Wallpaper Heart Pocket 147
Stuffed Grocery Bag Heart 148

Mobiles

Buttons and Bottle Caps Mobile 149
Gift Bows Mobile 150
Greeting Card Mobile 151
Styrofoam Fish Mobile 152
Paper Towel Roll Mobile 153

Storage

Jewelry Shoe Box 154
File Box Treasure Chest 155
Textured Coffee Cans 156
Bean Mosaic Cookie Can 157
Cereal Box Magazine Holders 158
Twine Wrapped Jars 159
Drink Bottle Candy Dispensers 160

Introduction

Make environmental responsibility fun with the projects in this book. Have children collect recyclable materials to make over 100 craft projects including garden tools, yard art, bird feeders, gifts, storage containers, and mobiles. Copy and provide each child with the Reuseable Materials List (page 6) to take home.

Make arts and crafts tools from plastic lids, Styrofoam trays, twist ties, old pens, cardboard, and hand towels.

Transform oatmeal boxes, soda bottles, and margarine tubs into bird feeders.

Help children make costumes from old T-shirts, tube socks, plastic milk containers and lids, and grocery bags.

Decorate rooms and walls with plastic butterflies, punched pie tin ornaments, detergent bottle and packing peanut sculptures, broken tile mosaics, crushed eggshell paintings, and clothing label collages.

Cut, color, and glue plastic lids, paint stirrers, egg cartons, and tuna cans for garden tools and yard art.

Organize craft supplies with file box treasure chests, cereal box magazine holders, and textured coffee cans.

Have children make gifts from coffee can lids, juice jars, blue jeans, old picture frames, and plastic milk bottles.

Create holiday displays, gifts, and decorations from old baseball caps, paper cups, wallpaper, grocery bags, plastic drink bottles, and egg cartons.

Reproduce the Eco-News format on page 10 for children to write about recycling, other environmental issues, or the projects they create. Then create an environmental awareness reference book. Decorate and write "Our Environmental Awareness" on the front of a loose leaf binder. Copy and insert the resource pages on pages 7-9 in the front of the book. Insert children's news forms in the binder along with photographs and articles about the environment.

Invite parents to attend an open house to view children's crafts from trash. Provide children with construction paper, crayons or markers, scissors, glue, and magazines. Have them make open house invitations for their families and friends.

Reuseable Materials List

Aluminum and Other Metals
  Coffee Cans*
  Aluminum Pie Tins*
  Aluminum Meal Tins*
  Aluminum Foil
Boxes
  Cereal Boxes
  Oatmeal Boxes
  Shoe Boxes
  Gift Boxes
  Small Appliance Boxes
  Shipping Boxes
  Empty Checkbook Boxes
Clothing and Linens
  Shoelaces
  T-shirts
  Socks
  Pillowcases
  Cutoff Pants or Slacks
  Mittens
  Gloves
Craft Supplies
  Popsicle Sticks*
  Yarn
  Empty Thread Spools
  Broken Cross Stitch Hoops
Miscellaneous
  Paint Stirrers
  Chop Sticks
  Wire Hangers
  Plastic Hangers
  Wallpaper Samples and Scraps
  Picture Frames
  Cocoa Mix Containers*
  Twist Ties

Paper and Cardboard
  Corrugated Board
  Cardboard from Laundered Shirts
  Newspapers
  Mat Board Scraps
  Paper Towel Tubes
  Food Wrap Tubes
  Expired Coupons
  Ribbon Scraps
  Gift Bows
  Greeting Cards
  Postcards
  Molded Cardboard Drink Holders
Plastics
  Styrofoam Meat Trays*
  Styrofoam Vegetable Trays*
  Margarine Tubs and Lids*
  Yogurt Containers and Lids*
  Plastic Foam Packing Peanuts
  Bubble Wrap
  Plastic Detergent Bottles
  Plastic Dish Soap Containers
  Berry Baskets*
  Plastic Resealable Storage Bags
  Clear Plastic Salad Containers
Sewing and Related Items
  Used Ribbon
  Rickrack Scraps
  Safety Pins
  Cloth Scraps
  Buttons
  Empty Thread Spools

* These items should be washed with soap and water.

Environmental Issues

Acid rain refers to the high acid content in precipitation of all kinds—rain, snow, and fog. Sulfur dioxide and nitrogen oxide are released into the atmosphere from industrial and power plants, automobile exhausts, and burning vegetation. These chemicals mix with rain droplets and form damaging acids. Acid rain affects lakes, man-made structures, and forests.

The damaging results are endless. Lakes and soil become contaminated; fish die and native wildlife suffers from a diminished food supply. The effect of acid rain leads to an endangered ecosystem.

Deforestation is directly associated with global warming, threatened species, and natural habitats. There are many different types of forests around the world. However, many forests support only one kind of ecosystem with the exception of the tropical rain forest, ancient forests, and dry forests. These three forests support many ecosystems or life cycles. Each year the earth loses millions of acres of forests that maintain ecosystems, produce 40% of the world's oxygen supply, and regulate the earth's climates. Deforestation also results in the dangerous reduction and possible extinction of rare and ancient trees.

Endangered species refers to animals and plants that are threatened with danger or extinction. The loss of entire groups of animals or plants changes the balance of nature, altering food chains, climates, plant growth, and food supplies around the world.

Global warming is the term used by scientists to describe the effect of unbalanced amounts of gases found in the air around the earth. The air around the earth is a balanced mixture of oxygen and nitrogen, carbon dioxide, methane, and other gases. Some of these gases capture and hold warmth from the sun in the atmosphere, which is referred to as the greenhouse effect. Without these gases, the earth would become a cold planet. However, the industrial revolution and other human activities have created an imbalance of this mixture. Burning of forests, altering wild lands, chemical leaks from automobiles, and air conditioning increase the release of heat-trapping gases that affect the earth's atmosphere.

 **Ozone** is a form of oxygen which is constantly produced in the stratosphere. It is a compound of three oxygen atoms unlike the oxygen we breathe which contains two atoms. The ozone layer in the stratosphere is a protective layer that prevents most of the life-destroying ultraviolet rays from reaching the earth. The release of large quantities of carbon gases contributes to the damaging effects and depletion of the ozone. Sometime during the late 1900s, scientists discovered a hole the size of the United States in the ozone layer over Antarctica.

 **Recycling** saves energy, natural resources, and landfill space. Almost all aluminum, glass bottles, office paper, and newspaper can be recycled. Recycling just these materials would reduce mining, logging, the use of raw materials, and the amount of garbage generated. Paper waste is the largest portion of the United States' trash. Efforts to recycle office papers, cardboard, corrugated board, and other paper products have been initiated by many solid waste management organizations and paper mills.

 **Rain forests** around the world receive at least 100 inches (250 cm) of rain each year. These forests are multilevel ecosystems that serve as habitats for nearly 50% of the world's species. Plant life found in rain forests remains green all year and helps the environment by using the carbon dioxide gases released into the air and producing a large percentage of the world's oxygen supply. Sadly, millions of trees are cut away each year for timber and to make way for progress. Careless destruction of rain forests destroys habitats, endangers species, and increases the level of carbon dioxide, which contributes to the problem of global warming.

Things to Do to Make a Difference

- Repair toys.
- Consider using ceiling fans rather than your air conditioner.
- Wear a sweater or sweat shirt when it's chilly inside rather than turning up the heat.
- Reduce the amount of garbage you generate.
- Carpool, ride bikes, or walk whenever possible.
- Close doors to rooms seldom used.
- Turn off lights and appliances when not in use.
- Share publication subscriptions with friends.
- Use cloth dish towels instead of paper towels.
- Use cloth napkins instead of paper napkins.
- Buy products in recyclable containers, then recycle when empty.
- Shop smart! Look for the recycle symbol on packaging.
- Wash clothes in cold water.
- Dry clothes on a clothesline.
- Take baths instead of showers.
- Make sure water spigots are turned off.
- Turn off the water while brushing your teeth.
- Take shorter showers.
- Use a trigger nozzle on water hoses.
- Turn off faucet while washing dishes.
- Water the lawn only when it needs it.
- Separate recyclables from garbage and other trash.
- Recycle aluminum cans and containers.
- Plant a tree.
- Recycle newspapers.
- Use the blank side of used paper for notes.
- Post a chalkboard for messages rather than a note pad.
- Reuse Styrofoam egg cartons.
- Reuse plastic and paper bags.
- Use rechargeable batteries.
- Avoid using flea collars on your pets. Try adding garlic to their food instead.
- Mend clothes.
- Make a compost pile of yard trimmings.

Eco-News

Styrofoam Stencil and Template

Materials:
You will need clean Styrofoam vegetable and fruit trays, a marker, scissors, a craft knife, paper, pencil, and cellophane tape.

Create a stencil and template from a disposable Styrofoam tray. Use a marker to copy one of the shapes below onto a Styrofoam tray. Ask an adult to use a craft knife to carefully cut the shape to form a stencil and template. Draw your own outline shapes to make additional stencils and templates. Store your stencils and templates in resealable plastic bags.

Baby Food Jar Supply Storage

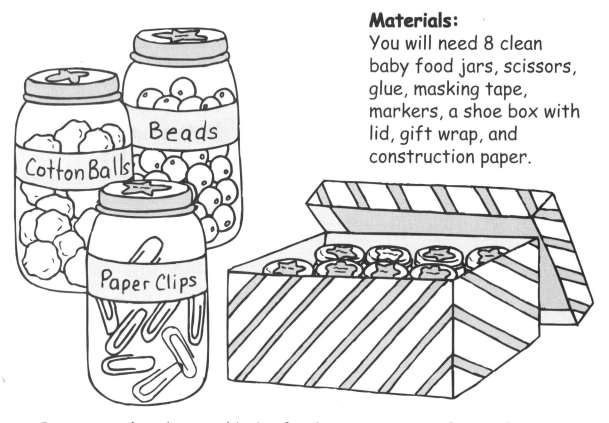

Materials:
You will need 8 clean baby food jars, scissors, glue, masking tape, markers, a shoe box with lid, gift wrap, and construction paper.

Convert a shoe box and baby food jars into a craft supplies storage unit. Cut and attach a strip of masking tape around each jar. Cut and glue a construction paper circle to the top of each lid. Copy one of the designs below onto each circle or create a design of your own. Then gather supplies such as buttons, beads, dried beans, game markers, paper clips, wiggly eyes, glitter, and other small craft supplies. Write the contents on the masking tape strip and lid of each jar. Cover a shoe box and lid with gift wrap or construction paper. Store your supply jars in the shoe box.

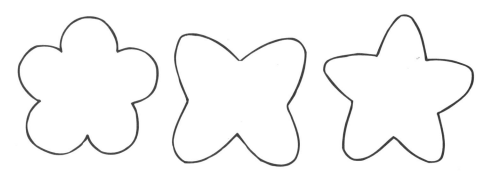

How to Make Crafts from Trash ©2002 Monday Morning Books, Inc.

Coffee Can Crayon Box

Materials:
You will need a clean coffee can with lid, gift wrap, scissors, glue, ribbon, yarn, and crayons.

Decorate a coffee can to store all of your crayons. Cut, measure, and glue gift wrap to fit around your coffee can. Glue ribbon or yarn around the can. Measure, cut, and glue a matching gift wrap circle to the lid. Fill your coffee can crayon box.

Plastic Lid Stencils and Templates

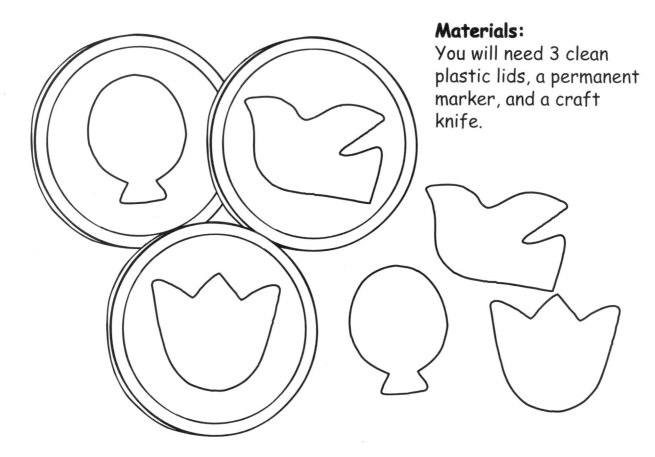

Materials:
You will need 3 clean plastic lids, a permanent marker, and a craft knife.

Make stencils and matching templates from plastic lids. Use a permanent marker to copy one of the shapes below onto a plastic lid. Ask an adult to use a craft knife to carefully cut the shape to form a stencil and template.

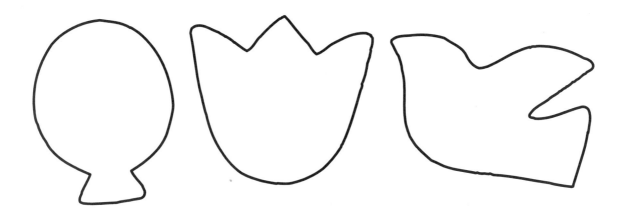

Dry Pen Scratching Tool

Materials:
You will need a dry ball point pen, masking tape, and permanent markers.

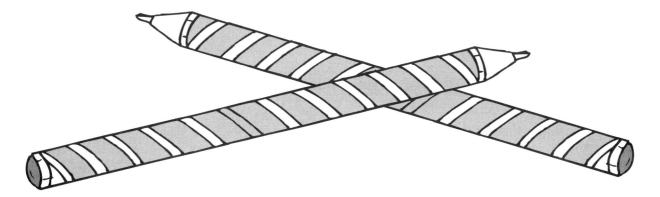

Dry ball point pens make great scratching tools. Use permanent markers to copy one of the designs below onto a strip of wide masking tape or create a design of your own. Wrap the masking tape around the pen barrel.

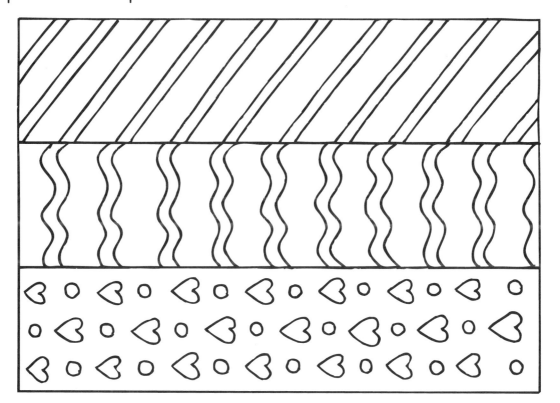

Yarn and Cardboard Portfolio

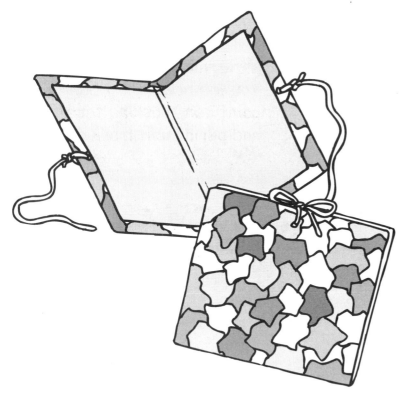

Materials:
You will need 2 sheets of cardboard, a ruler, a pencil, wide masking tape, scissors, a paintbrush, glue, craft tissue, gift wrap, a hole punch, and yarn.

Make a portfolio to store your photographs and drawings. Measure and cut two sheets of cardboard the same size. Place them side by side with a pencil between them as shown (A). Attach a strip of wide masking tape to hinge the two sheets of cardboard. Remove the pencil and attach another strip of masking tape to the opposite side (B).

Working with a small section at a time, use a paintbrush to apply glue, then attach torn craft tissue to one side of the hinged boards. Overlap the edges and glue tissue to the opposite side (C). Measure, cut, and glue a sheet of gift wrap to the inside of the portfolio (D). Punch a hole in the center of each outside edge. Tie a length of yarn through each hole. Place your papers inside the portfolio and tie the yarn into a bow.

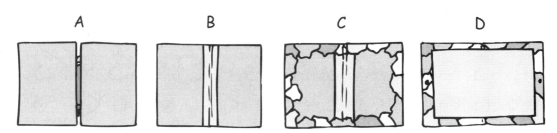

Hand Towel Paintbrush Wallet

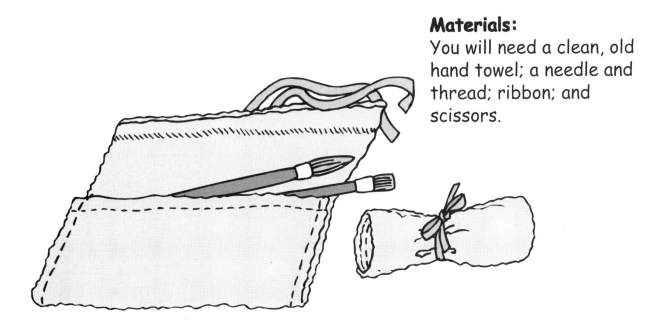

Materials:
You will need a clean, old hand towel; a needle and thread; ribbon; and scissors.

Make a wallet from an old hand towel. Cut a hand towel in half and stitch a hem along the cut edge (A). Fold over the stitched edge to form a pocket and sew along the short ends (B). Cut, fold in half, and stitch a ribbon to the flap (C). Place your paintbrushes in the wallet pocket. Then wrap the flap and ribbon ties around the wallet and tie a bow.

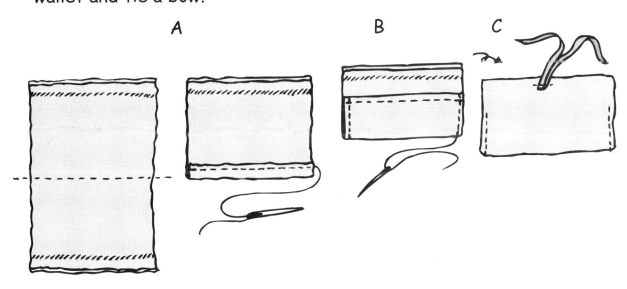

A   B   C

Glitter Dispensers

Materials:
You will need dish soap dispensers, construction paper, glue, markers or crayons, scissors, and glitter.

Store glitter in decorative dish soap dispensers. Copy the labels on this page onto construction paper or create designs of your own. Color, cut out, and glue the labels to your glitter dispensers. Fill the dispensers with glitter.

Mustard Bottle Paint Dispensers

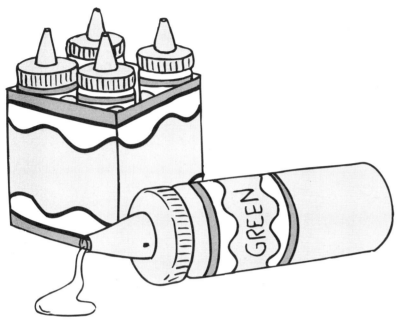

Materials:
You will need clean mustard bottles, tempera paint, construction paper, crayons or markers, scissors, cellophane tape, and a square tissue box

Store your tempera paint in easy-to-dispense mustard bottles. Copy, color, and cut out the label below for each bottle or create one of your own. Write the matching color word on the label. Then wrap and tape the label around the bottle. Make additional paint dispensers for other colors. Fill the bottles with tempera paint.

Transform a square tissue box into a storage bin for your paint dispensers. Cut away the top of a square tissue box. Measure, decorate, cut, and glue a sheet of construction paper around the tissue box. Place your paint dispensers in the box. Make additional storage boxes to hold more dispensers.

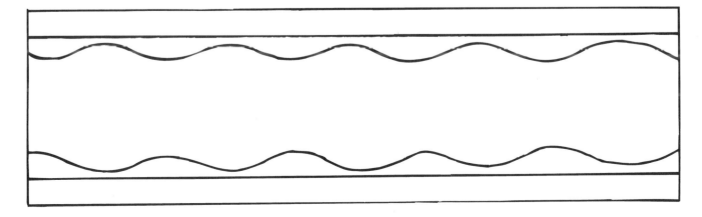

Sponge Stamps

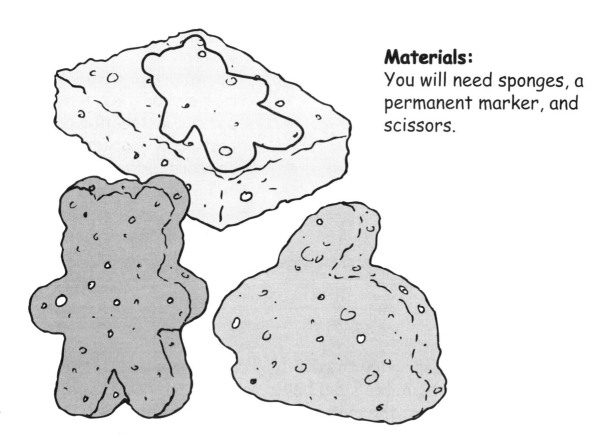

Materials:
You will need sponges, a permanent marker, and scissors.

Use sponge stamps to stencil gift wrap, book covers, storage boxes, and more. Use a permanent marker to copy one of the shapes below onto a dry sponge or create an outline design of your own. Carefully cut out the shape.

How to Make Crafts from Trash ©2002 Monday Morning Books, Inc.

Old Plate Palette

Materials:
You will need an old plate, masking tape, and permanent markers.

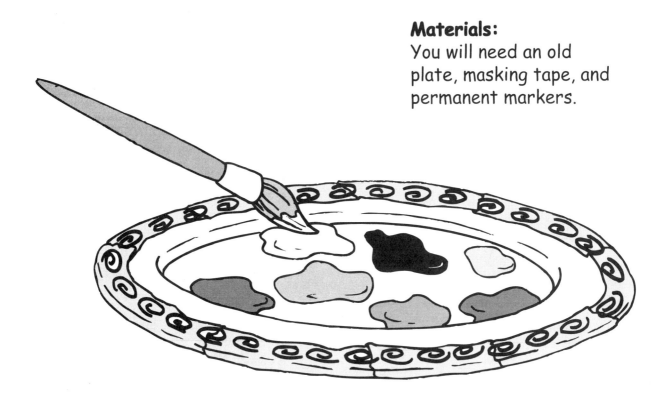

Mix colors on a fancy personalized palette. Carefully wrap the edge of a plate with masking tape. This will make it easy to grip the plate while you mix your colors. Use permanent markers to decorate the masking tape. Replace and decorate the masking tape edge when it becomes worn.

Twist Tie Needles

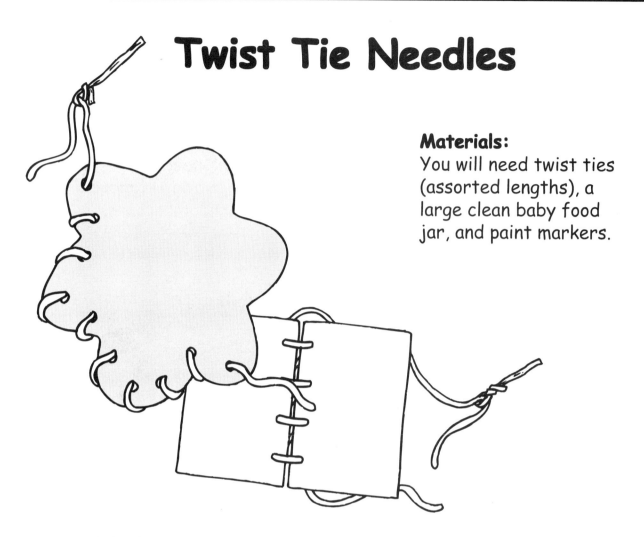

Materials:
You will need twist ties (assorted lengths), a large clean baby food jar, and paint markers.

Make lacing and sewing paper or cardboard safe and easy with twist tie needles. Bend and twist a twist tie to form an eye (A). Thread yarn, twine, or ribbon through the eye. Long twist ties are great for sewing paper towel tubes together (B). Use paint markers to decorate a large baby food jar and lid. Store your twist ties in the jar.

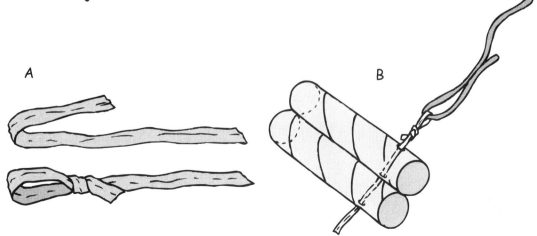

A   B

Plastic Lid Texture Tools

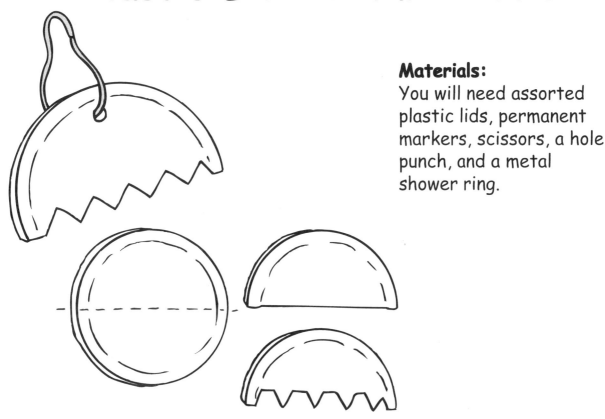

Materials:
You will need assorted plastic lids, permanent markers, scissors, a hole punch, and a metal shower ring.

Use cut plastic lids to create unusual patterns when you paint. Cut a plastic lid in half as shown. Copy and cut one of the texture patterns below along the straight edge of a plastic lid half (above). Copy another texture pattern onto the remaining half lid. Punch a hole along the rounded edge of each tool. Thread each tool onto a metal shower ring. To use a texture tool: Drag the tool across a wet, painted surface in a straight, zigzag, or swirling motion.

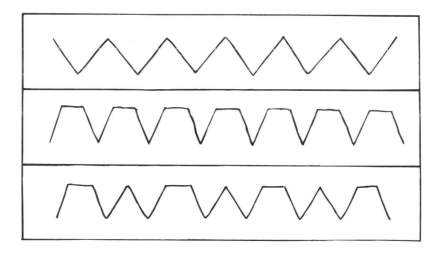

Cardboard Weaving Loom

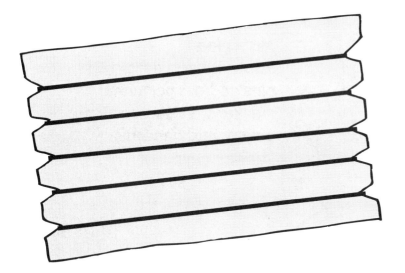

Materials:
You will need a sheet of corrugated board, scissors, twine or rug yarn, masking tape, a long twist tie needle, and a craft stick.

Make a portable weaving loom from a corrugated board and yarn. Cut an odd number of triangle notches along opposite edges of a sheet of corrugated board as shown above. Use masking tape to secure a length of twine or rug yarn to the center of the board (A). Lace twine between the notches (B). Cut and secure the twine to the board with tape (C). Use a twist tie needle to weave yarn over and under the twine (D). Use a craft stick to tighten the space between the woven yarn (E). When you have finished weaving, cut the yarn, then tie each loose end around one of the lengths of twine on the loom.

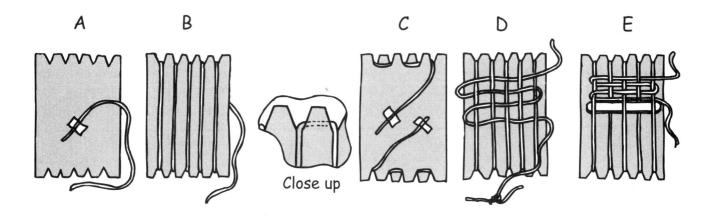

A   B   C   D   E

Close up

Jar Lid Pin Cushion

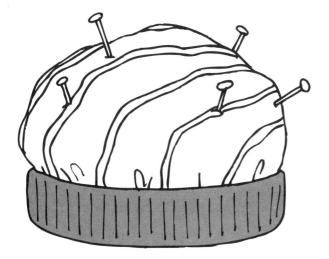

Materials:
You will need a clean jar lid, cardboard, scissors, fabric scraps, quilt batting, glue, and a marker.

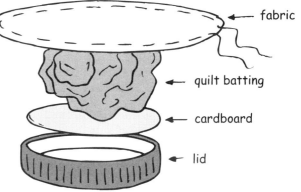

fabric

quilt batting

cardboard

lid

Make a beautiful jar lid pin cushion for yourself or as a gift. Measure and cut a cardboard circle to fit inside the jar lid. Cut a fabric circle twice the size of the cardboard insert. Use a needle and thread to sew around the edges of the fabric circle leaving a length of thread at the beginning and the end as shown below (A). Place a wad of quilt batting in the center of the fabric circle. Pull the thread ends and form a cushion (B). Apply glue to one side of the cardboard circle. Position the cushion, stitched side down, on the cardboard circle (C). Apply glue and press the cushion inside the lid (D).

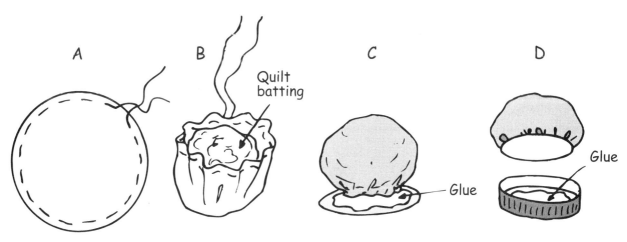

A

B   Quilt batting

C   Glue

D   Glue

Soda Bottle Feeder

Materials:
You will need a clean plastic soda bottle, scissors, permanent marker, twine or yarn, and bird seed.

Make a bird feeder from a plastic soda bottle. Draw an oval about the size of a wallet photo on the side of a small soda bottle. Ask an adult to use a pair of scissors or a craft knife to cut out the oval. Ask your adult helper to use a craft knife to cut two small holes below the mouth of the bottle as shown. Lace and tie a length of yarn or twine through the holes as shown. Fill the bottle with bird seed and hang on a branch.

Straw Hat Feeder

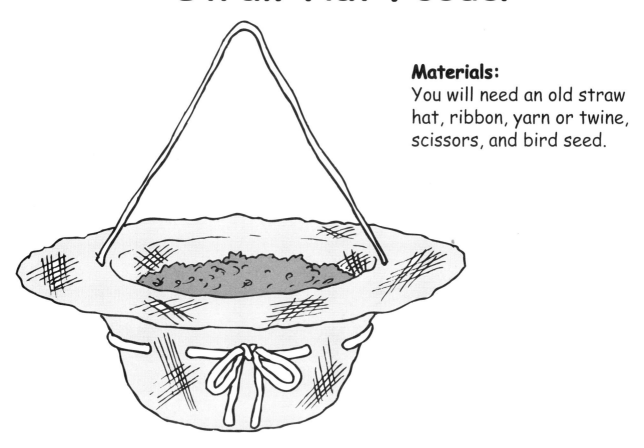

Materials:
You will need an old straw hat, ribbon, yarn or twine, scissors, and bird seed.

Transform an old straw hat into an attractive bird feeder. Punch an odd number of holes around the crown of the hat (A). Lace and tie a ribbon through the holes and tie the ends into a bow. Punch two holes at opposite sides of the crown (B). Lace and tie a length of yarn or twine through the holes for hanging. Fill the crown with bird seed and hang it from a tree branch.

A   B

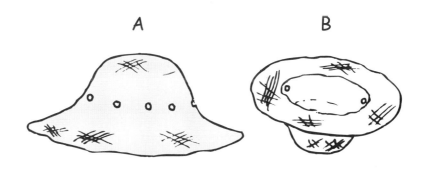

Margarine Tub Feeder

Materials:
You will need a clean margarine tub and lid, glue, scissors, permanent markers, yarn or twine, and bird seed.

Make a small bird feeder from a margarine tub. Ask an adult to cut a small round opening in the side of the margarine tub as shown above. Then have your adult helper cut two small holes on opposite sides of the tub just below the rim. Lace and tie a length of yarn or twine through the holes. Decorate the tub with permanent markers. Fill the tub with bird seed. Place the lid on the tub and hang it from a branch.

Oatmeal Container Bird Feeder

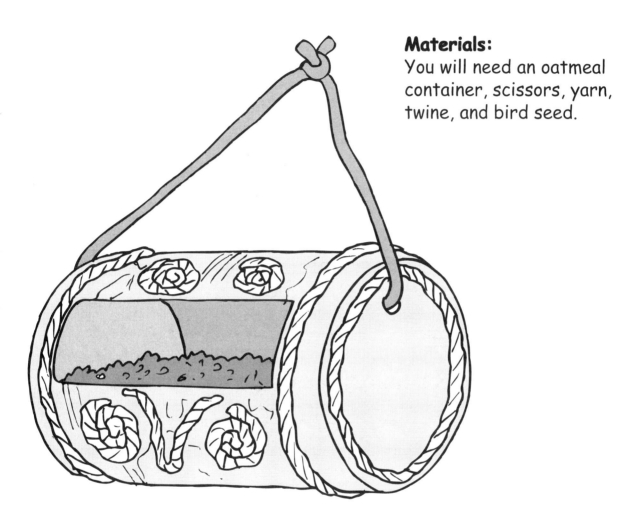

Materials:
You will need an oatmeal container, scissors, yarn, twine, and bird seed.

Transform a disposable oatmeal container into a handy bird feeder. Ask an adult to cut an opening in the side of the container as shown above. Decorate the outside of the container with yarn. Punch a hole in the lid and the bottom of the container. Lace and tie a length of twine through the holes. Fill the container with bird seed and hang it from a tree branch.

Egg Carton Feeder

Materials:
You will need a clean Styrofoam egg carton, scissors, markers, yarn or twine, and bird seed.

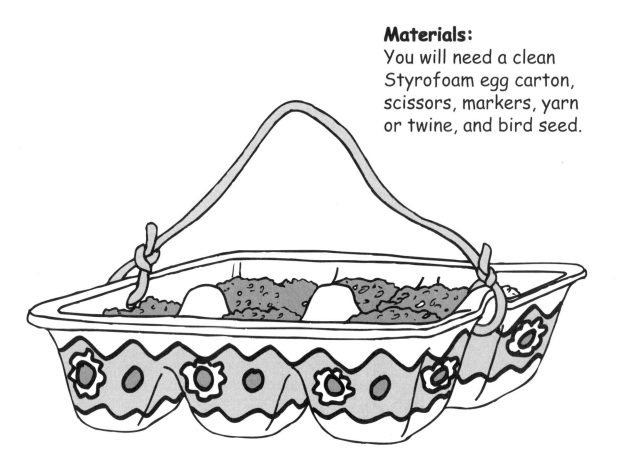

Make a bird feeder from a Styrofoam egg carton. Cut a Styrofoam egg carton in half. Use markers to decorate the outside of the carton. Punch two holes at each narrow end of the carton as shown. Cut and tie the loose ends of a length of yarn through each hole. Fill the carton with bird seed and hang it from a branch.

Flower Pot Feeder

Materials:
You will need an old clay flower pot and dish, ribbon, yarn, and bird seed.

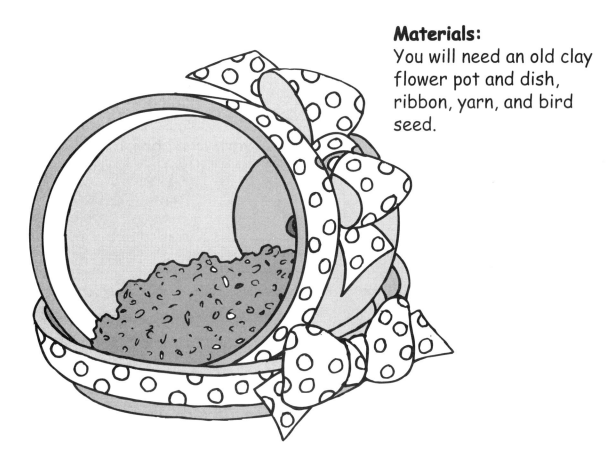

Transform an old clay flower pot and dish into a fancy bird feeder to place in your backyard. Measure, cut, and tie a length of ribbon around the rim of the pot and the dish. Tie the loose ends into a bow. Place the flower pot in the dish as shown above. Pour bird seed inside the pot and place the feeder outside.

Styrofoam Tiger Mask

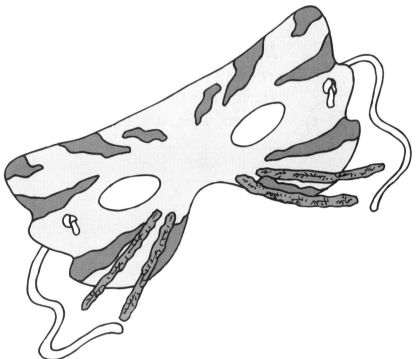

Materials:
You will need a large Styrofoam vegetable tray, black and orange markers, scissors, and yarn or ribbon.

Make a tiger mask from a clean Styrofoam vegetable tray. Copy the tiger mask shape below onto a Styrofoam tray. Cut out the mask and eye holes. Use orange and black markers to color the mask. Punch two holes in the mask and tie a length of yarn or ribbon through each hole.

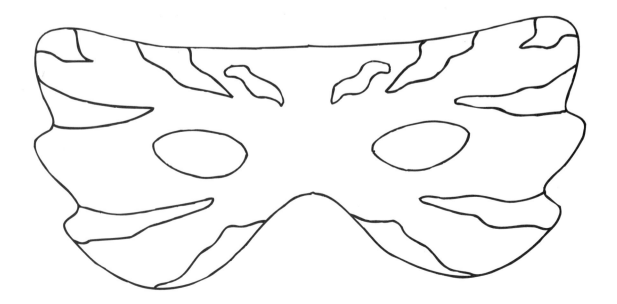

How to Make Crafts from Trash ©2002 Monday Morning Books, Inc.

Tiger Stripes T-shirt

Materials:
You will need an old, white T-shirt; and black and orange fabric markers.

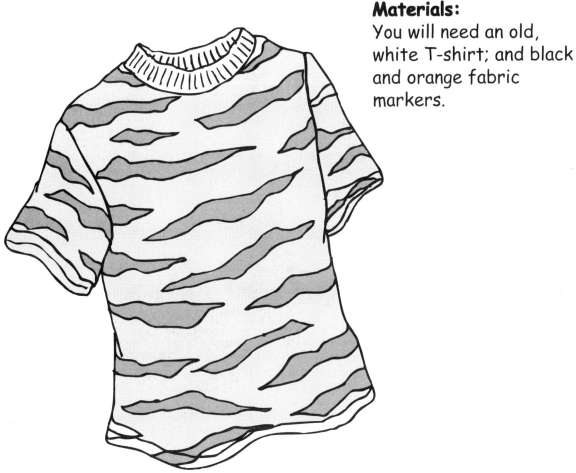

Create a tiger stripe T-shirt to wear with a Styrofoam tiger mask. Use a black fabric marker to draw and fill in stripe shapes on your T-shirt. Then use an orange marker to color the rest of the T-shirt.

Tiger Stripe Socks

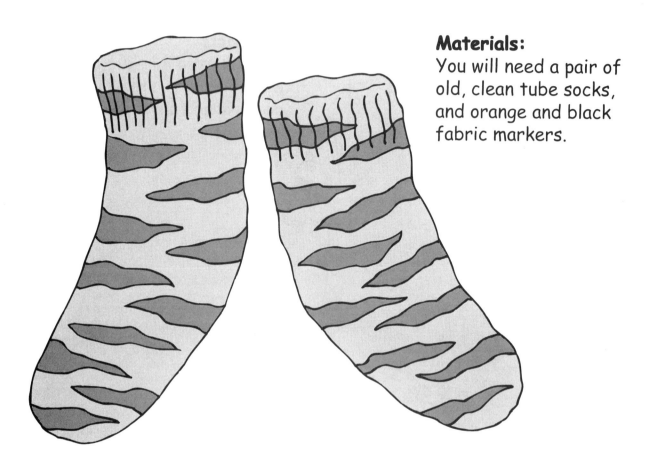

Materials:
You will need a pair of old, clean tube socks, and orange and black fabric markers.

Complete your tiger costume with these tiger stripe socks to match your tiger mask and T-shirt (pages 32-33). Use a black fabric marker to draw and fill in stripe shapes on each sock. Then color the rest of each sock with an orange fabric marker.

Styrofoam Fish Mask

Materials:
You will need a large, Styrofoam vegetable tray, markers, scissors, and yarn or ribbon.

Make a fish mask from a clean Styrofoam vegetable tray. Copy the fish shape below onto a Styrofoam tray. Cut out the mask and eye holes. Use markers to color the mask. Punch two holes in the mask and tie a length of yarn or ribbon through each hole.

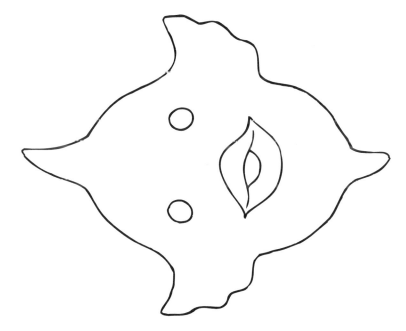

Plastic Lid Fish Scale T-shirt

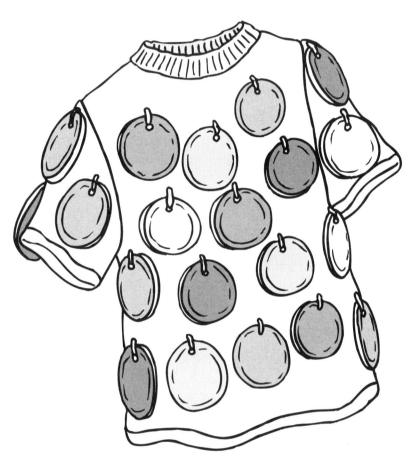

Materials:
You will need small, white or clear plastic lids; old, white T-shirt; permanent markers; scissors; hole punch; sewing needle; and heavy thread.

Create a fish scale T-shirt to wear with a Styrofoam fish mask. Punch a hole along the edge of each lid. Use permanent markers to color the lids. Then sew each lid to your T-shirt with a needle and heavy thread.

Styrofoam Bird Mask

Materials:
You will need a large, Styrofoam vegetable tray, markers, scissors, and yarn or ribbon.

Make a bird mask from a clean Styrofoam vegetable tray. Copy the bird mask shape below onto a Styrofoam tray. Cut out the mask and eye holes. Use markers to color the mask. Punch two holes in the mask and tie a length of yarn or ribbon through each hole.

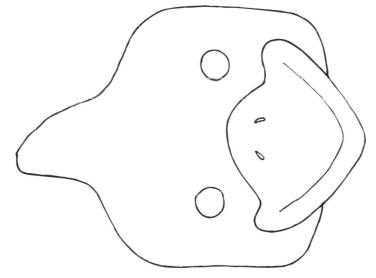

Feather T-shirt

Materials:
You will need an old, white T-shirt; and fabric markers.

Create a feather T-shirt to match a Styrofoam bird mask. Use fabric markers to draw feather shapes on your T-shirt as shown above.

Styrofoam Elephant Mask

Materials:
You will need a large, Styrofoam vegetable tray, brown marker, scissors, and yarn or ribbon.

Make an elephant mask from a clean Styrofoam vegetable tray. Copy the elephant mask shape below onto a Styrofoam tray. Cut out the mask and eye holes. Use a brown marker to color the mask. Punch two holes in the mask and tie a length of yarn or ribbon through each hole.

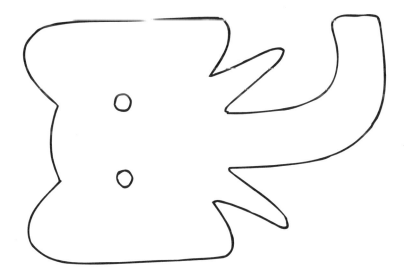

Grocery Bag Elephant Vest

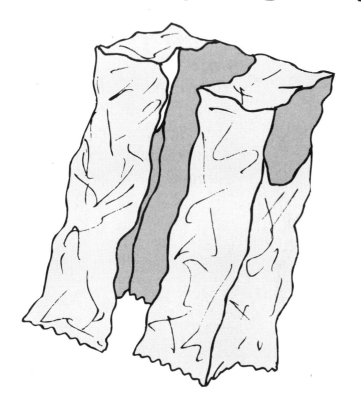

Materials:
You will need a brown grocery bag and scissors.

Create a grocery bag elephant vest to wear with a Styrofoam elephant mask. Crumple a brown grocery bag, then smooth it out to create a wrinkle effect. Cut an opening, a neck hole, and two arm holes as shown below.

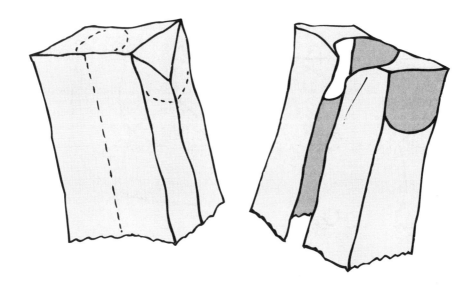

How to Make Crafts from Trash ©2002 Monday Morning Books, Inc.

Elephant Toe Socks

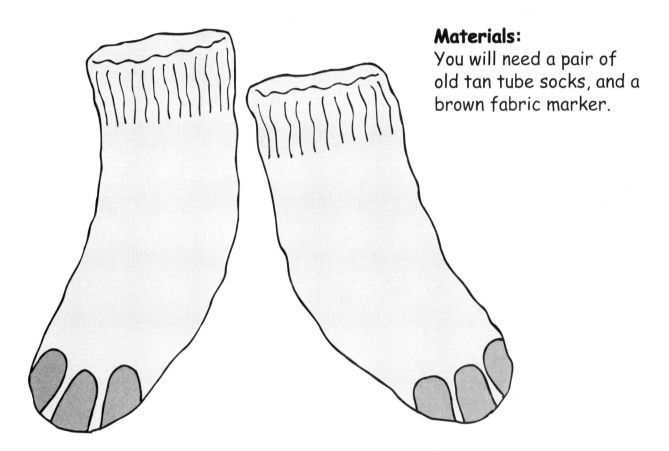

Materials:
You will need a pair of old tan tube socks, and a brown fabric marker.

Complete your elephant costume with these elephant toe socks to match your elephant mask and vest (pages 39-40). Then use a brown fabric marker to draw three elephant toes on each sock.

Space Creature Mask

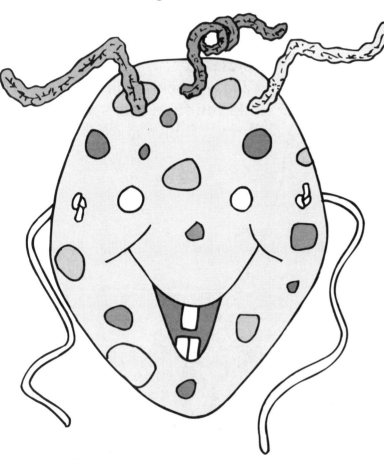

Materials:
You will need a large, Styrofoam vegetable tray, markers, pipe cleaners, buttons, glue, scissors, and yarn or ribbon.

Make a space creature mask from a clean Styrofoam vegetable tray. Copy the space creature shape below onto a Styrofoam tray or design one of your own. Cut out the mask and eye holes. Use markers, pipe cleaners, and buttons to decorate your mask. Punch two holes in the mask and tie a length of yarn or ribbon through each hole.

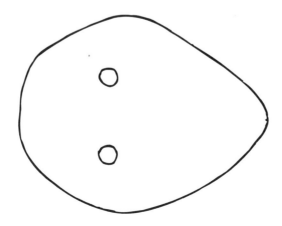

Bubble Wrap Vest

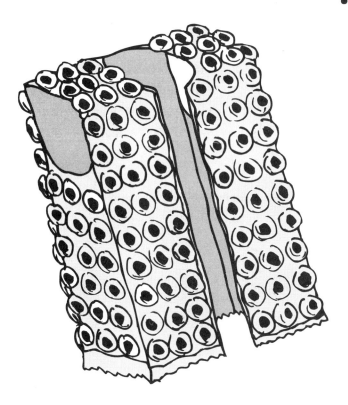

Materials:
You will need a brown grocery bag, bubble wrap, markers, scissors, cellophane tape, and a stapler.

Turn a grocery bag and bubble wrap into part of your space creature costume. Cut an opening, a neck hole, and two arm holes as shown. Measure, cut, and tape or staple bubble wrap to the bag. Use markers to add color to your bubble wrap vest.

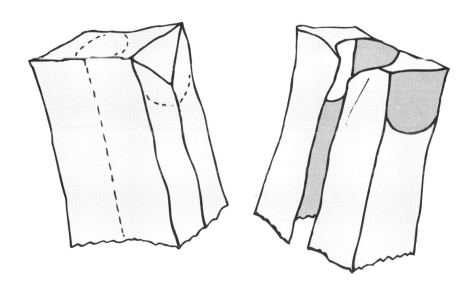

Alien Sock Feet

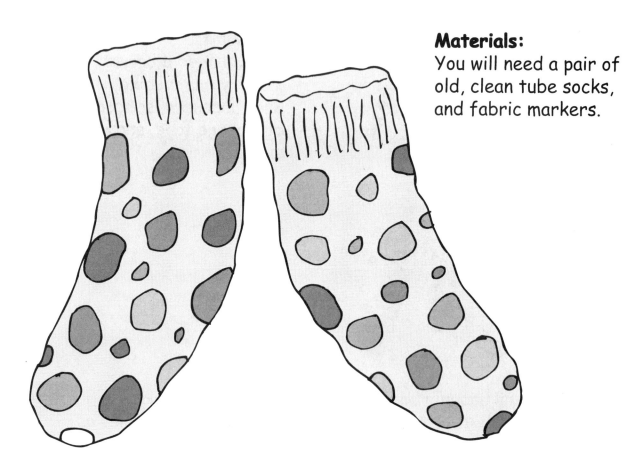

Materials:
You will need a pair of
old, clean tube socks,
and fabric markers.

Make a pair of alien socks to match your space creature mask
and bubble vest (pages 42-43). Use fabric markers to decorate
each sock.

Milk Container Helmet

Materials:
You will need a large plastic milk container, construction paper, masking tape, scissors, and permanent markers.

Make a helmet from a clean plastic milk container. Cut out the bottom and an opening in the milk container (A). Copy, cut, and tape a strip of fringed construction paper around the top of the container (B). Use permanent markers to decorate your helmet.

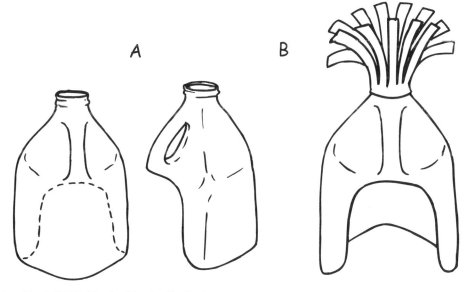

A   B

Pillow Case Knight's Tunic

Materials:
You will need a solid color pillow case; scissors, yarn, and fabric markers.

Make a knight's tunic from an old pillow case. Cut a neck and two arm holes in the pillow case as shown. Use fabric markers to draw one or more of the designs below on your tunic. Measure and cut a length of yarn to use as a belt.

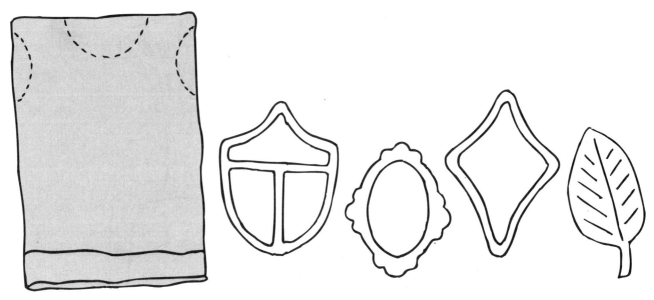

How to Make Crafts from Trash ©2002 Monday Morning Books, Inc.

Knight Boots

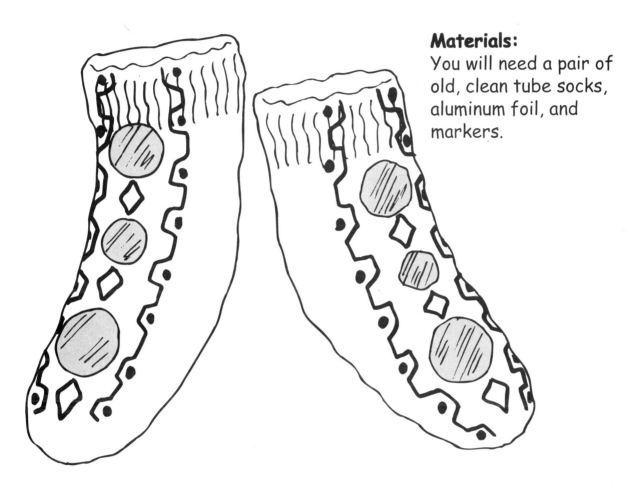

Materials:
You will need a pair of old, clean tube socks, aluminum foil, and markers.

Complete your knight costume with a pair of knight boots made from old tube socks and aluminum foil. Decorate each sock with matching designs from your tunic and helmet (pages 45-46). Then cut and glue aluminum foil circles to the front of each sock.

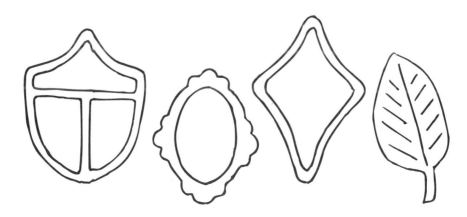

Plastic Milk Container Butterflies

Materials:
You will need a clean plastic milk container, scissors, permanent or paint markers, hole punch, and pipe cleaners.

Make two butterfly decorations from plastic milk containers. Cut a plastic milk container as shown below. Use a permanent marker to copy the butterfly pattern below onto one of the milk container corner sheets. Cut out and decorate the butterfly with paint markers. Punch two holes, lace a pipe cleaner, and curve the ends as shown. Repeat these steps to make a second butterfly.

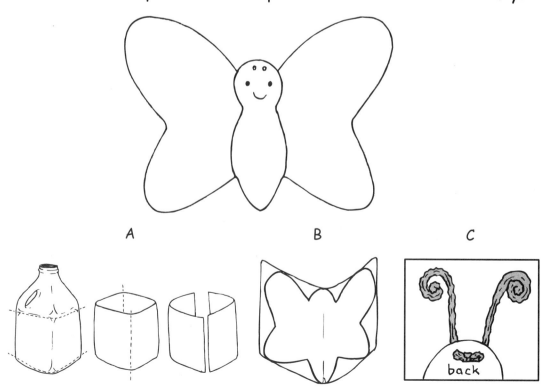

A   B   C

back

Plastic Grocery Bag Bunnies

Materials:
You will need 2 plastic grocery bags, and permanent markers.

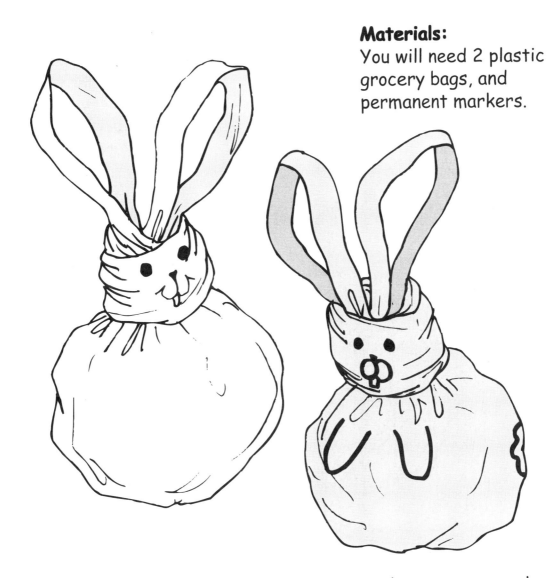

All you need is two plastic grocery bags and permanent markers to make each of these delightful bunnies. Stuff a plastic grocery bag with a second plastic bag. This will form the bunny's body. Pull the handles together and tie a knot above the stuffed portion of the bag. This will form the bunny's head. Pull up and separate the handles to form the bunny's ears. Use a permanent marker to draw a face and other details.

Bottle Character

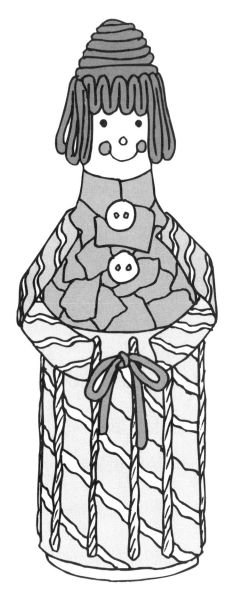

Materials:
You will need a clean bottle, fabric scraps, scissors, glue, yarn, buttons, ribbon, and paint markers.

Make a bottle character from a clean empty bottle. Use paint markers to draw a face at the top of the bottle. Cut and glue yarn hair at the top of the bottle. Measure, cut, and glue cloth around the bottom half of the bottle. Then cut and glue overlapping fabric patches for a shirt. Allow the glue to dry. For slacks, draw a line to designate separate pant legs. Cut and glue a rectangle fabric arm to either side of the bottle. You can glue the fabric arms in different positions. Decorate your bottle character with buttons, yarn, and ribbon.

Jar Lid Wind Chimes

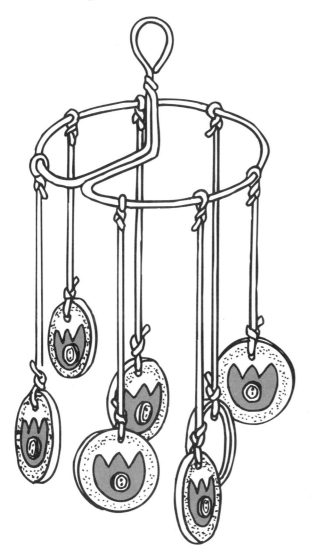

Materials:

You will need a wire hanger, assorted metal jar lids, nail and hammer, paint markers, construction paper, scissors, glue, sequins, buttons, beans, glitter, and yarn.

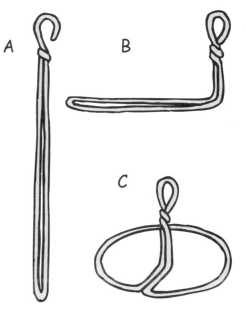

Ask an adult to help you bend a wire hanger into a circular shape as shown here. Decorate your jar lids with construction paper cutouts, buttons, sequins, paint markers, and glitter. Ask your adult helper to use a hammer and nail to punch a hole along the edge of each lid. Measure and cut lengths of yarn to tie to each of your lids. Then tie the loose ends around the circle hanger. Hang your jar lid wind chime outside.

Egg Carton Flowers

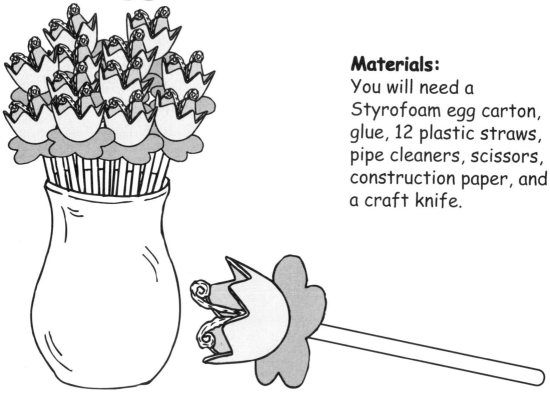

Materials:
You will need a Styrofoam egg carton, glue, 12 plastic straws, pipe cleaners, scissors, construction paper, and a craft knife.

Make a bouquet of beautiful egg carton cup flowers. Cut out the cups from pink, blue, white, or yellow Styrofoam egg cartons. Then cut the rim of each cup (A). Copy and cut out construction paper flowers shown here. Cut a small hole in the bottom of each cup and in the center of each flower (B). Assemble and apply glue to each flower (C). When the glue has dried, cut, bend, and glue a pipe cleaner inside the cup as shown. Make a dozen flowers to place in a flower vase.

Detergent Bottle Sculpture

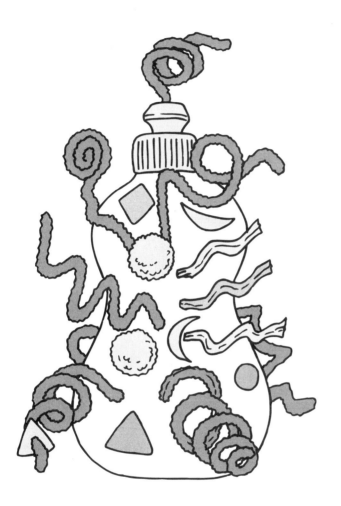

Materials:

You will need a clean dry detergent bottle, twist ties, construction paper, permanent markers, pompoms, scissors, yarn, glue, buttons, pipe cleaners, and small bottle caps.

Create an amazing detergent bottle sculpture decoration. Use permanent markers to draw designs on a clean and dry detergent bottle. Ask an adult helper to use a craft knife to punch several holes in your bottle. Twist and bend pipe cleaners and twist ties to insert in the holes. Finish decorating your bottle sculpture with construction paper shapes, yarn, and buttons.

Terra Cotta Flower Pot People

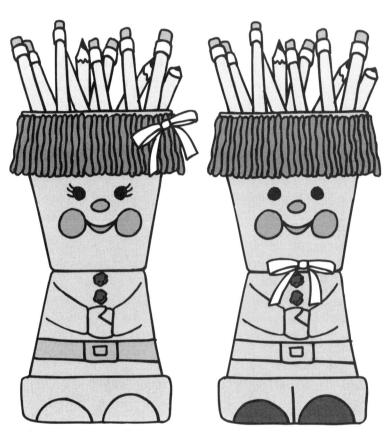

Materials:
You will need 2 to 3 discarded clay pots, glue, white and yellow felt, scissors, paint markers, 2 small black pompoms, yarn, yellow rickrack or ribbon, acrylic paint, and paintbrushes.

Make flower pot people to display in a garden or as room decorations. Glue two clay pots together, end to end as shown. Use a paint marker to draw arms, legs, shoes, and a belt on your clay pot figure. Glue pompom buttons to the front. Cut and glue yarn around the top of your figure for hair. Use acrylic paint to add eyes, a nose, a mouth, and cheeks. Glue a ribbon hair bow or bow tie to your terra cotta character.

Pie Tin Punch Ornament

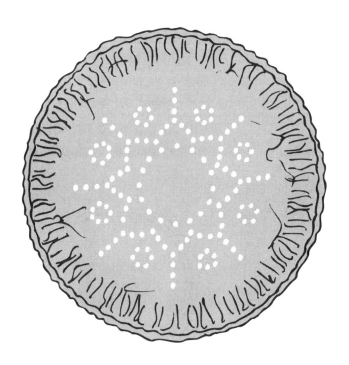

Materials:
You will need a small aluminum pie tin, newspaper, a sheet of corrugated cardboard, paper, a large paper clip or a scratching tool, and yarn.

Make an attractive aluminum pie tin ornament to hang in a window or on the wall. Cover a flat surface with several layers of newspaper. Then place a sheet of corrugated cardboard on the newspaper. Flatten a clean aluminum pie tin on the cardboard. Copy the pattern here onto a sheet of paper or create one of your own. Tape the pattern over the flattened pie tin. Unbend a large paper clip or use a scratching tool, to punch each dot, piercing through the paper and the pie tin. Remove the paper, then punch a hole at the top of the tin. Lace and tie a length of yarn through the hole for hanging.

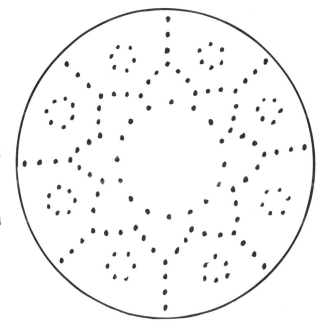

Plastic Lid Refrigerator Magnet

Materials:
You will need a plastic lid, a ruler, gift wrap, scissors, glue, buttons, ribbon, pasta noodles, markers, and magnetic tape.

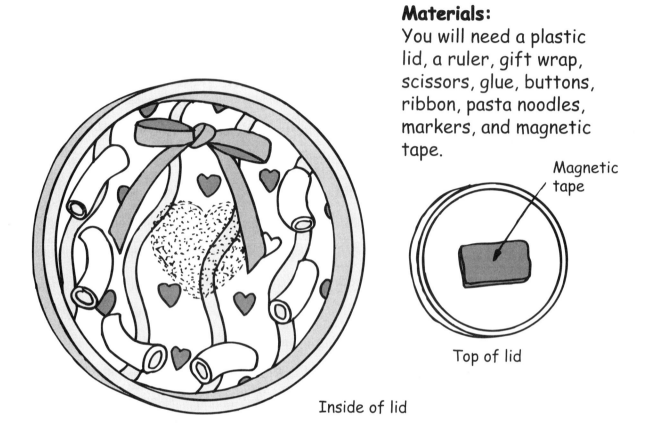

Magnetic tape

Top of lid

Inside of lid

Make your own magnet to secure notes, coupons, and artwork to your refrigerator. Measure and cut a gift wrap circle to fit inside a plastic lid. Decorate your lid with buttons, ribbon bows, or pasta noodles. Cut and attach a strip of magnetic tape to the top of the lid.

How to Make Crafts from Trash ©2002 Monday Morning Books, Inc.

Resealable Bag Sun Catcher

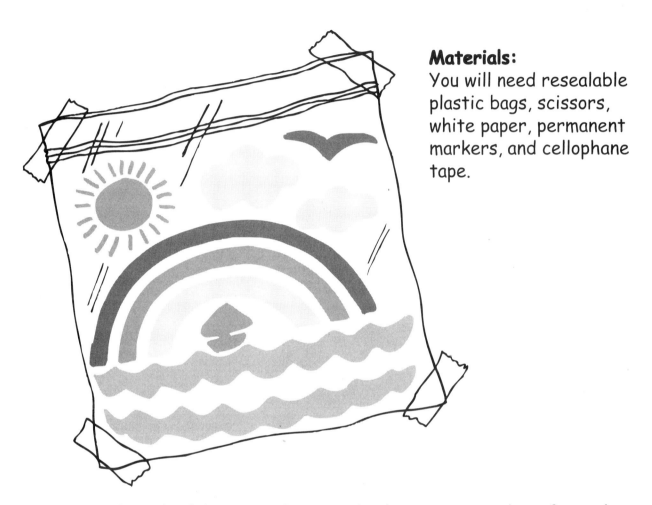

Materials:
You will need resealable plastic bags, scissors, white paper, permanent markers, and cellophane tape.

Make colorful sun catchers to display in your windows from clean resealable plastic bags. Measure and cut a sheet of white paper to fit inside a resealable plastic bag. Draw a picture on the paper. Slide the paper inside the plastic bag. Then use permanent markers to trace and color your picture onto the plastic bag. Remove your paper drawing. Use cellophane tape to attach your sun catcher to a window.

Broken Flower Pot Nature Collage

Materials:
You will need newspapers, a broken clay pot, scissors, corrugated cardboard, markers, glue, dry leaves, twigs, acorns, twine, ribbon, and pipe cleaners. Note: Handle broken edges with care.

Make a collage with a broken clay pot and a variety of craft supplies. Cover a table with several layers of newspaper. Cut a circle from a sheet of corrugated cardboard. Use markers to decorate the cardboard circle. Apply glue to the clay pot and place it on the cardboard. Allow the glue to dry. Then glue twigs, twisted pipe cleaners, acorns, twine, and dry leaves inside and around the pot. Cut, tie, and glue a ribbon bow to the pot.

Artificial Flower Collage

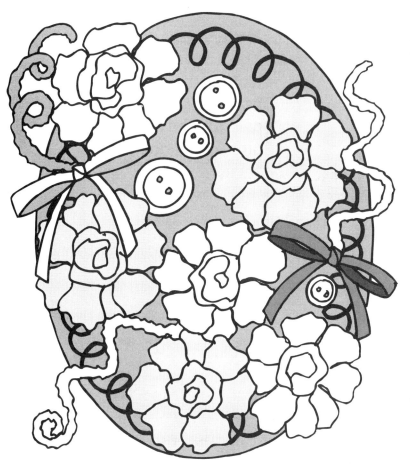

Materials:
You will need a sheet of corrugated cardboard, scissors, glue, pipe cleaners, ribbon, buttons, markers, and a variety of artificial flowers.

Make an attractive display from corrugated cardboard and artificial flowers. Cut a sheet of corrugated board into an oval. Use markers to decorate the cardboard. Cut and glue artificial flowers, pipe cleaners, buttons, and ribbon bows to the decorated board.

Old Clothing Appliques

Materials:
You will need old clothing fabric scraps, a permanent marker, a pair of scissors, straight pins, and a needle and thread.

Make sew-on appliques from old clothing fabric scraps. Use a permanent marker to draw one of the patterns below onto a fabric scrap or create a shape of your own. Cut out and pin the applique to a pair of pants, socks, a jacket, skirt, or shirt. Sew on the applique with a needle and thread.

Plastic Collar Critter

Materials:
You will need a plastic lid, scissors, paint markers, wiggly eyes, pipe cleaners, glue, and glitter.

Make a collar critter from a plastic lid. Cut a flap in the center of each lid as shown. Use paint markers to color the lid. Glue on wiggly eyes, and pipe cleaners shaped into ears, legs, or antennae. Add sparkle to your critter with glue and glitter.

Plastic Hair Ornament

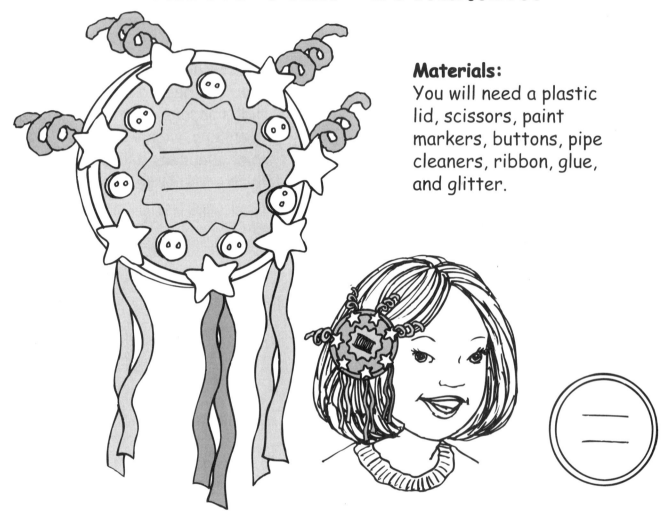

Materials:
You will need a plastic lid, scissors, paint markers, buttons, pipe cleaners, ribbon, glue, and glitter.

Create a beautiful, funny, or glittery ornament to wear in your hair. Cut two slits in the center of the lid as shown. Use paint markers to decorate the lid. Glue on ribbon bows, buttons, or cork screw pipe cleaners. Add sparkle to your hair ornaments with glue and glitter.

Drink Can Holder Collage

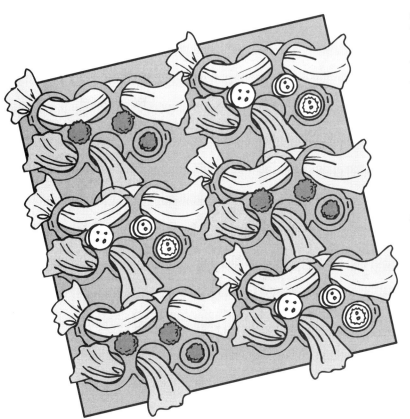

Materials:
You will need a large sheet of corrugated cardboard, paint, paintbrush, several plastic drink can holders, cloth scraps, pompoms, buttons, markers, scissors, glue, and a stapler.

Paint a sheet of corrugated cardboard. Staple plastic drink can holders to the board. Weave cloth scraps through the plastic rings. Glue on pompoms and buttons. Use markers to add decorative details.

Cereal Box Village

Materials:
You will need empty
cereal boxes,
construction paper, gift
wrap scraps, scissors,
glue, and markers

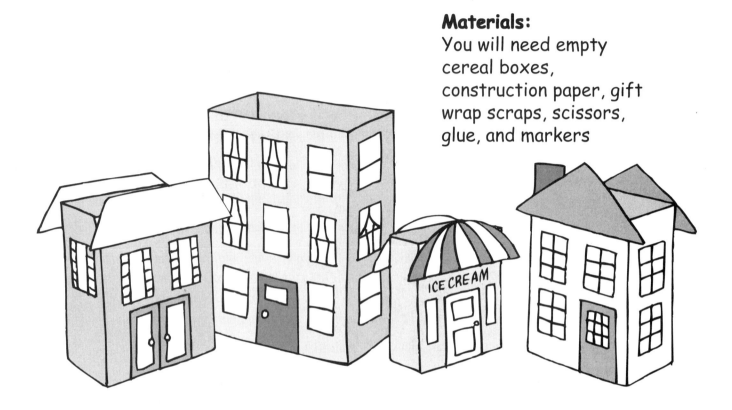

Create a cereal box village for display or to use in a play area.
Measure, cut, and glue construction paper to each cereal box. Cut
rectangle windows, shutters, and doors to glue onto each cereal
box building. Cut and glue gift wrap curtains to each window. Use
markers to add details such as window panes, door knobs and
shingles, and shutter slats.

How to Make Crafts from Trash ©2002 Monday Morning Books, Inc.

Broken Tile Mosaic

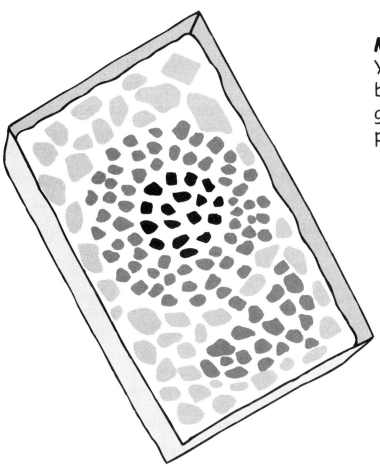

Materials:
You will need a shoe box, broken tile, scissors, glue, a small bag of plaster, and a sponge.

Make a colorful broken tile mosaic. Cover a worktable with newspaper. First arrange the tile to make a design, then glue each piece of tile inside a shoe box lid. Allow the glue to dry. Mix plaster in a small container according to the directions on the bag. Fill the spaces between the broken tile with the plaster mixture. Use a moist sponge to wipe excess plaster from the tile.

Woven Necktie Wall Hanging

Materials:
You will need old neckties, 2 wooden dowels, yarn, a needle, and thread.

Make a unique wall hanging from old neckties. Fold and stitch a loop at each end of five ties as shown. Slide a dowel through the loops at each end of the five ties as shown to form a loom. Then, starting at the bottom, weave one tie at a time through the loom.

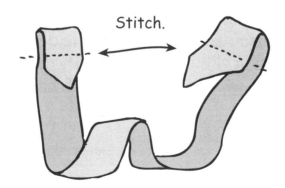

Stitch.

Checkbook Box Collector's Display

Materials:
You will need empty checkbook boxes, construction paper, scissors, glue, wide masking tape, and markers.

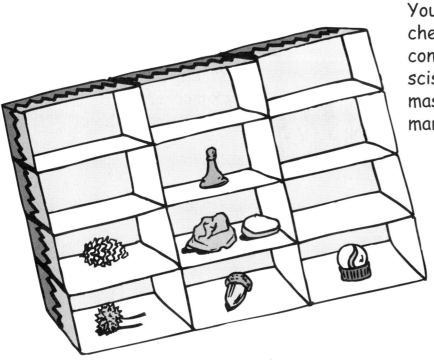

Make a multi-compartment collector's display from empty checkbook boxes. Measure, cut, and glue construction paper to the inside of each box. Glue the boxes together to form a display case as shown above. Wrap wide masking tape around the sides of the assembled display case. Then use markers to decorate the masking tape. Place small items such as rocks, old game pieces, and small toys in your display case.

Berry Basket Dry Flower Display

Materials:
You will need a berry basket, scissors, dry flowers, yellow construction paper, black marker, pipe cleaners, and ribbon.

Make a small dry flower arrangement to display on a bookshelf, table, or dresser. Copy, then cut out two yellow construction paper bees (below). Glue each bee to a pipe cleaner. Cut and insert dry flowers in an upside down berry basket. Insert the pipe cleaner bees between the flowers. Cut and tie ribbon bows. Then wrap a pipe cleaner around the center of each bow and insert them between the flowers.

Scrap Wire Sculpture

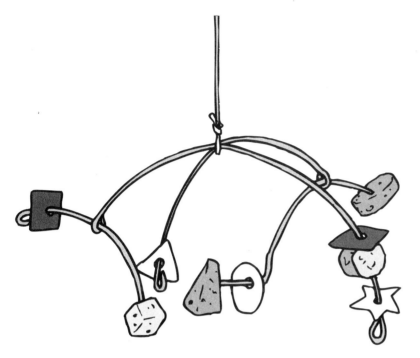

Materials:
You will need discarded wire hangers, wire cutters, pliers, scissors, hole punch, poster board scraps, buttons, aluminum foil, and sponges.

Make a fun sculpture with the supplies listed above and your imagination. Cut shapes from poster board and sponges. Ask an adult to help you cut and bend wire. Punch a hole in poster board shapes to slide onto wires. Carefully punch sponge shapes onto wire ends or slide wire through the sponge shapes. Move the poster board and sponge shapes to adjust the balance of each wire.

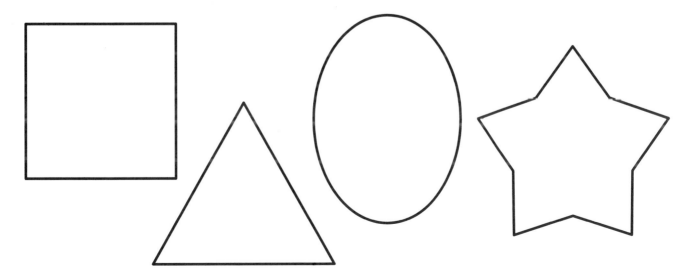

Crushed Eggshell Painting

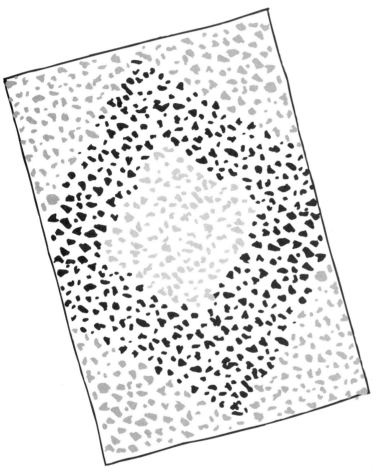

Materials:
You will need clean eggshells, a plastic bag, paint, a paintbrush, poster board, and glue.

Create a textured painting using clean crushed eggshells and paint. Wash and dry eggshells. Place and crush the shells inside a plastic bag. Use a paintbrush to apply glue to a poster board. Then press crushed eggshells into the glue. When the glue has dried, paint a picture or design on the eggshell covered poster board.

Artificial Flowers Window Display

Materials:
You will need a discarded broomstick, glue, scissors, wide ribbon, artificial flowers, and curtain rod brackets.

Make a decorative display to hang from the top of a window. Cut and glue wide ribbon strips to a broomstick. Cut off the stems from artificial flowers. Glue a flower to each loose ribbon. Ask an adult to help you hang your flower rod over a window.

Paper Towel Tube 3-D Collage

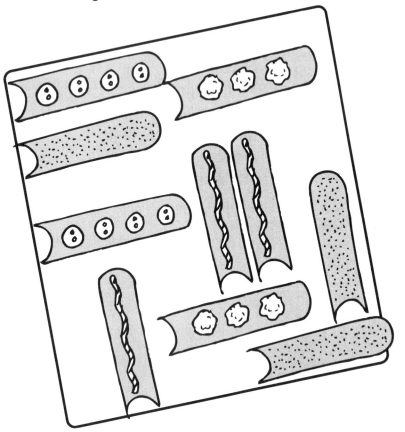

Materials:
You will need paper towel tubes, scissors, markers, beans, beads, pasta noodles, buttons, pipe cleaners, pompoms, glitter, yarn, and poster board.

Make an unusual 3-D collage using paper towel tubes and a variety of craft supplies. Cut your paper towel tubes in half as shown (A). Decorate the tubes with the craft supplies listed above. Apply glue to the edges of each tube and glue them onto a sheet of poster board.

A

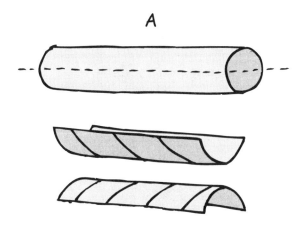

How to Make Crafts from Trash ©2002 Monday Morning Books, Inc.

Packing Peanuts Sculpture

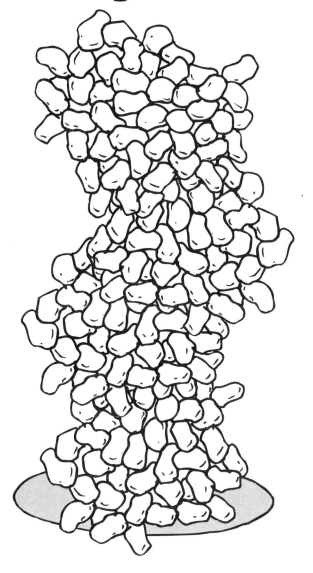

Materials:
You will need packing peanuts, a corrugated board circle, black construction paper, and glue.

Create a modern art sculpture using packing peanuts and glue. Measure, cut, and glue a black sheet of construction paper to one side of a corrugated board circle. Apply glue to packing peanuts and attach to the center of the black circle stand. Continue gluing packing peanuts to form your sculpture. If you are making a tall sculpture, work in levels and allow glue to dry before adding another level.

Tissue and Oatmeal Box Robot

Materials:
You will need empty tissue and oatmeal boxes, aluminum foil, construction paper, bottle caps, jar lids, pompoms, craft sticks, crayons or markers, scissors, pipe cleaners, wiggly eyes, and glue.

Make a robot colony from oatmeal and tissue boxes. Measure, cut, and glue construction paper to the outside of each oatmeal or tissue box. Then use a marker to draw a head and face on each box. Glue assorted bottle caps, aluminum foil shapes, jar lids and pipe cleaners to your robot. Use craft sticks or pipe cleaners for arms, legs, fingers, or toes. Draw additional details with crayons or markers.

Tissue Boxcars

Materials:
You will need empty tissue boxes, metal jar lids, construction paper, scissors, glue, crayons or markers, magazines, and grocery store advertisements.

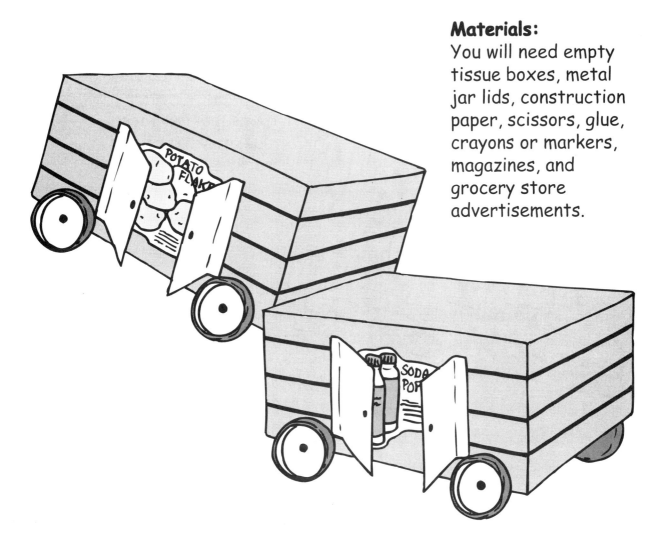

Make boxcars from tissue boxes. Measure, cut, and glue construction paper to each tissue box. Glue four jar lid wheels to the tissue box as shown above. Cut construction paper doors. Fold a tab along one edge of each door pattern. Apply glue and align the doors on the boxcar. Glue magazine and grocery store advertisement cutouts under each set of doors.

Clothing Label Collage

Materials:
You will need clothing labels cut from old, throwaway clothing items, poster board, glue, and crayons or markers.

Make a collage with cutout clothing labels. First, decide what size poster board you want to work on. Arrange your labels on a sheet of poster board. When you have finished arranging the labels in the design or pattern you want, lift each label, apply glue to the back, and place it back on the board. Continue doing this until all the labels have been glued to the board. Use crayons or markers to finish your collage.

Styrofoam Tray Scrimshaw

Materials:
You will need a clean Styrofoam fruit or vegetable tray, a scratching tool, tempera paint, a shallow container, paintbrush, scissors, and a sponge.

Make a unique display to hang on a wall or display on a desk. Use a large paper clip or scratching tool to draw a picture or design on a clean Styrofoam tray. When you are done scratching your design, choose a color and paint your design. Do not allow the paint to dry completely. While slightly wet, gently wipe excess paint from the tray with a moist sponge. Do not wipe the paint from the scratch lines.

Molded Drink-Holder 3-D Painting

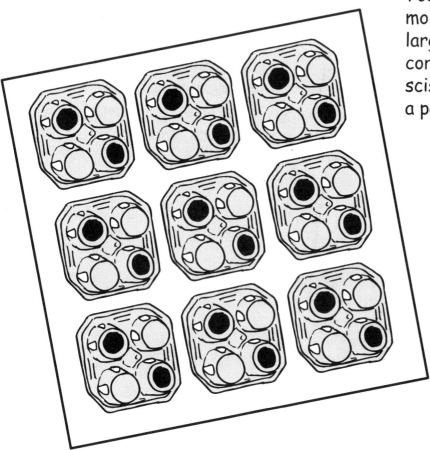

Materials:
You will need several molded drink-holders, a large sheet of corrugated cardboard, scissors, glue, paint, and a paintbrush.

Make a colorful 3-D painting to hang on your wall. Glue molded drink-holders to a large sheet of corrugated cardboard. Paint each cup a separate color or alternate the colors to create a patterned design.

Plastic Lid Bumble Bees

Materials:
You will need clean plastic lids, yellow and white construction paper, a black marker, scissors, glue, pipe cleaners, a hole punch, fishing line, and pushpins.

Make plastic lid bumble bees to hang in a window or from the ceiling. Measure, cut, and glue a yellow construction paper circle to a plastic lid. Use a black marker to draw stripes on the circle. Cut out and glue a yellow construction paper head and white wings to the lid. Bend and glue pipe cleaner antennae on the bee's head. Punch a hole and tie a length of fishing line to the bee. Tie the loose end of the fishing line around the stem of a pushpin. Then hang the bee in a window or from the ceiling.

Potting Soil Scoops

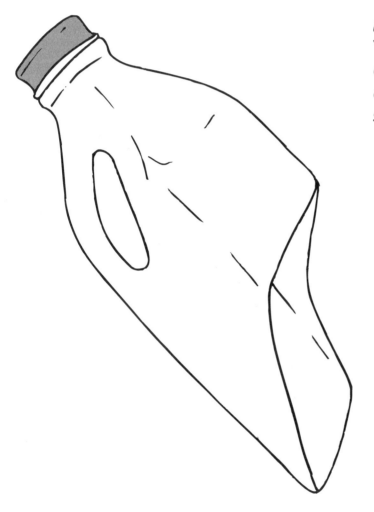

Materials:
You will need plastic
drink bottles and milk
containers with lids and
scissors.

Make soil scoops from different size plastic drink and milk
bottles. Cut the bottom from a clean drink bottle or milk container.
Then cut away a slanted portion from the bottle as shown above.

Paint Stirrer Plant Stakes

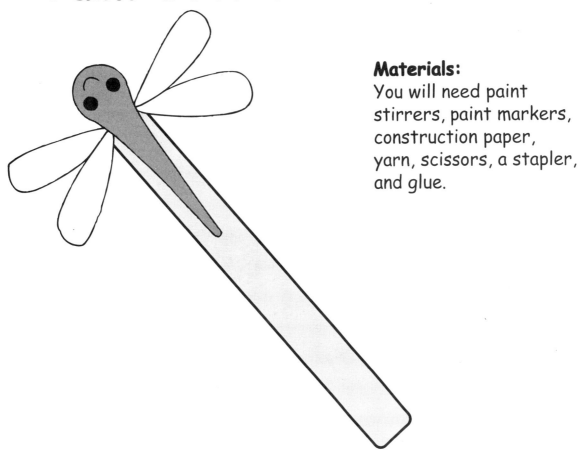

Materials:
You will need paint
stirrers, paint markers,
construction paper,
yarn, scissors, a stapler,
and glue.

Make plant stakes from paint stirrers and construction paper.
Copy, color, cut out, and staple one of the patterns below to one
end of a paint stirrer or design a pattern of your own. Place the
stake in a plant.

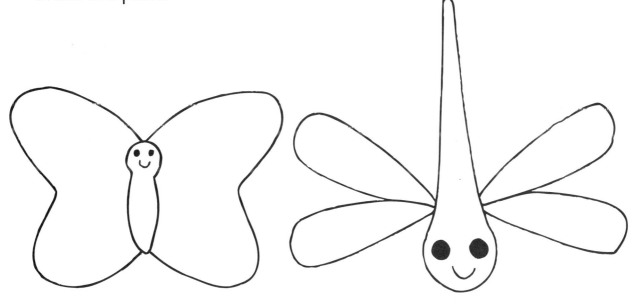

Egg Carton Seed Planters

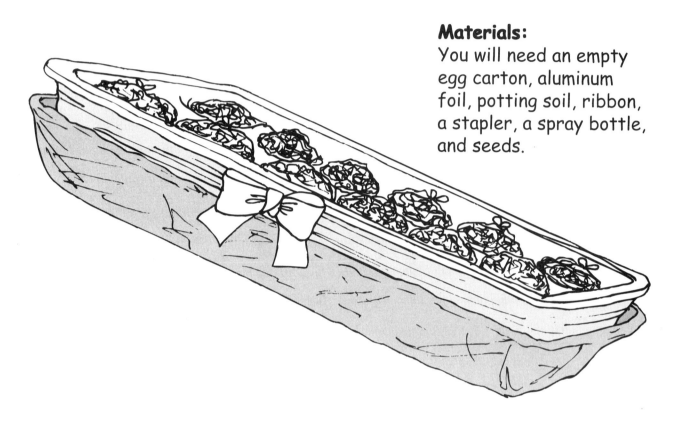

Materials:
You will need an empty egg carton, aluminum foil, potting soil, ribbon, a stapler, a spray bottle, and seeds.

Start plants from seeds in an egg carton. Carefully cut off the top of the egg carton. Wrap the outside of the cover with aluminum foil and place the egg cup section inside. Measure, cut, and staple a length of ribbon around the outside of the planter. Tie a length of ribbon into a bow and staple it to the planter. Fill each cup with soil. Use your thumb to form a well in each soil-filled cup. Spray water in each cup. Then place and cover the seeds in each with soil. Place your egg carton planter where it can get plenty of sunlight. Spray water on your planter every day.

Soda Bottle Bird Seed Scoops

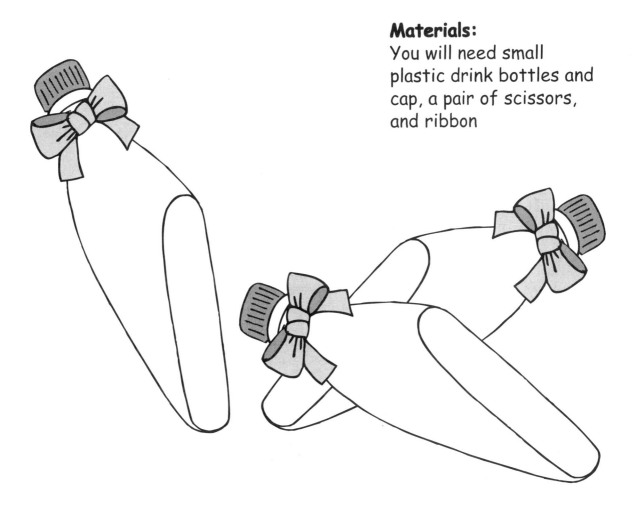

Materials:
You will need small plastic drink bottles and cap, a pair of scissors, and ribbon

Make decorative bird seed scoops from small plastic drink bottles. Cut the bottom from a clean drink bottle. Then cut away a slanted portion from the bottle as shown above. Screw on the cap, then cut and tie a ribbon bow around the neck of the bottle.

Wind Wigglers

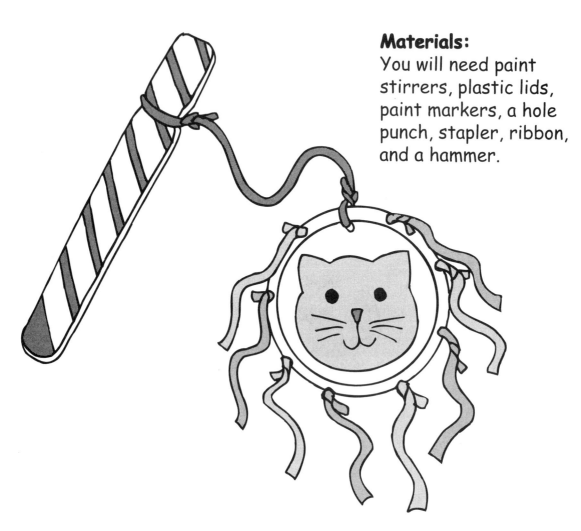

Materials:
You will need paint stirrers, plastic lids, paint markers, a hole punch, stapler, ribbon, and a hammer.

Make wind wigglers to place in your yard or garden. Use paint markers to decorate a paint stirrer and a plastic lid. Punch holes around the edge of the lid and tie ribbon through each hole as shown above. Wrap and staple a length of yarn to the lid and the paint stirrer. Use a hammer to gently drive the wind wiggler in the ground.

Paint Can Tool Carrier

Materials:
You will need a clean paint can, construction paper, stickers, yarn, scissors, crayons, markers, and glue.

Store and carry your tools in a colorful paint can. Measure, cut, and glue construction paper around a paint can. Cut and glue construction paper shapes, stickers, or yarn to your tool can. Add decorative details with crayons and markers.

Cream Cheese Planter

Materials:
You will need a clean cream cheese container, paint markers, a large plastic lid, a nail, and a hammer.

Make a cream cheese container planter for a small plant such as a cactus or violet. Decorate the outside of a cream cheese container with paint markers. Ask an adult to use a nail and hammer to punch 4 holes in the bottom of the can. Plant a cactus or violet in your planter. Place the planter on a plastic lid, then water and place your plant where it can receive sunlight.

Bottle Cap Checkers

Materials:
You will need 32 bottle caps, paint markers, poster board, and a ruler.

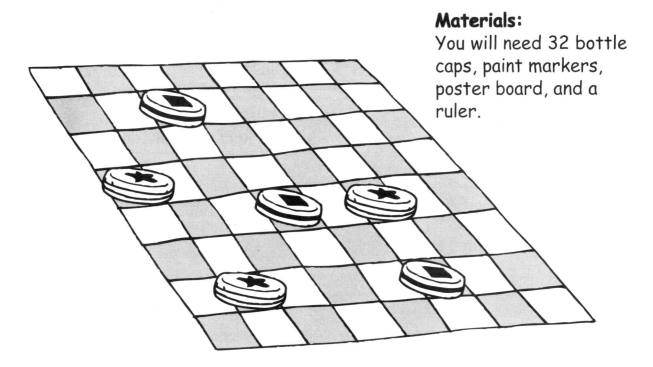

Make your own checker board game with bottle caps and poster board. Measure and cut a sheet of poster board into a square. Use a ruler to measure 8 equal columns on the poster board square in each direction as shown above. Then color every other block on the board. Use paint markers to decorate 16 bottle caps with the same design. Decorate the remaining 16 caps with a different design. Set up your board and ask a friend to play a friendly game of bottle cap checkers.

Coffee Can Lid Fan

Materials:

You will need a large plastic coffee can lid, a large craft stick or paint stirrer, paint markers, ribbon, and a stapler.

Make a colorful hand-held fan from a coffee can lid. Use paint markers to decorate both sides of a large plastic coffee can lid. Staple the lid to a large craft stick or paint stirrer. Tie a ribbon bow at the base of the fan.

Craft Tissue Juice Jar Vases

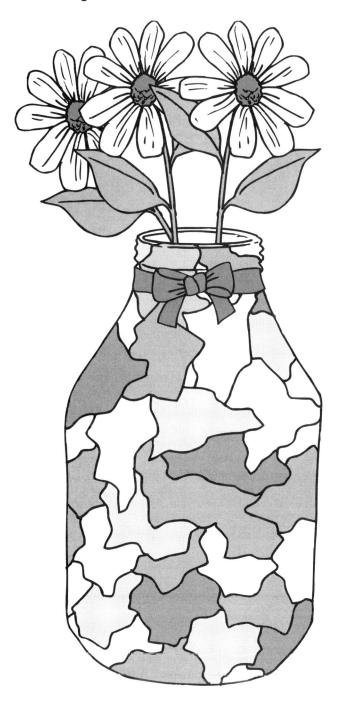

Materials:
You will need craft tissue, glue, a paintbrush, a clean juice jar, and ribbon.

Transform a juice jar into a beautiful vase. Tear and glue craft tissue to the bottle. Allow the glue to dry. Then cut and tie a ribbon bow around the top of the vase.

Artsy Soap Dispenser

Materials:
You will need a soap dispenser and paint markers.

Make a special gift from a soap dispenser decorated with paint markers. Copy one of the designs below or create one of your own.

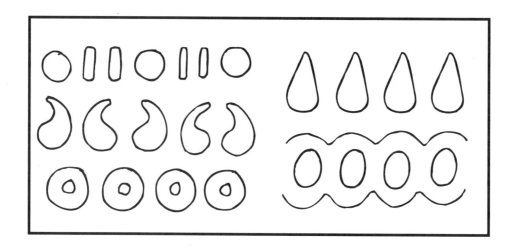

Wallpaper Keepsake Boxes

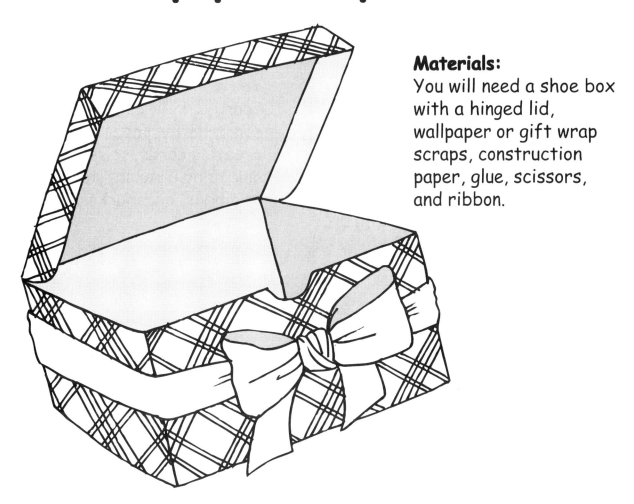

Materials:
You will need a shoe box with a hinged lid, wallpaper or gift wrap scraps, construction paper, glue, scissors, and ribbon.

Transform a shoe box into a keepsake box with wallpaper scraps and ribbon. Measure, cut, and glue gift wrap or wallpaper to the outside of a shoe box. Then measure, cut, and glue construction paper to the inside of the box and lid. Cut, wrap, and tie a ribbon bow around the center of the box as shown above.

Note: If you do not have a hinged lid shoe box, cut a slit in two corner of the lid. Attach the lid to the box with a strip of wide masking tape before decorating.

Greeting Card Scrapbook

Materials:
You will need poster board, gift wrap or construction paper, old greeting cards, scissors, glue, a hole punch, yarn or ribbon, and markers.

Make a scrapbook to display your family's greeting cards. Measure and cut two poster board covers to match the size of your construction paper. Punch two holes along the left side of each page and cover. Lace and tie yarn or ribbon through each hole to form a booklet. Use markers to decorate the cover, then glue your greeting cards in your scrapbook.

Memory Stones in a Jar

Materials:
You will need a clean peanut butter jar and lid and paint markers.

Collect and display memory stones in a peanut butter jar. Use paint markers to write "My Memory Stones" and decorate a clean peanut butter jar. Collect a stone from each place you visit or one to remind you of an event, holiday, or person. Place your stones in your memory jar. Share the story of each stone with a friend or your family.

Paper Towel Tube Napkin Rings

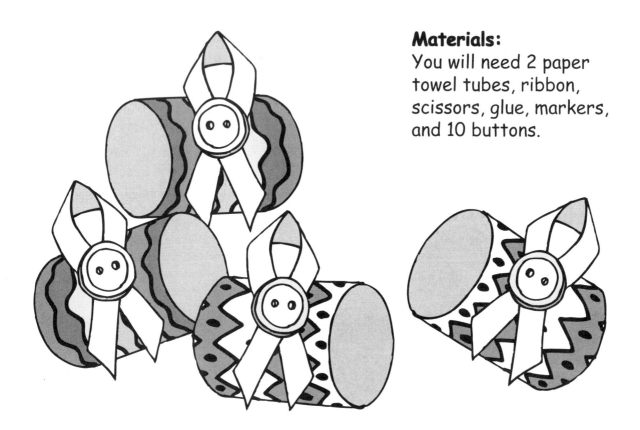

Materials:
You will need 2 paper towel tubes, ribbon, scissors, glue, markers, and 10 buttons.

Make 10 matching napkin rings from two paper towel tubes. Measure and cut each paper towel tube into five equal size rings. Use markers to decorate and color the rings. Measure, cut, and glue ribbon around each ring. Then cut and glue a ribbon loop and button to each ring as shown above.

Yarn-Wrapped Picture Frame

Materials:
You will need an old picture frame, scissors, a paintbrush, glue, and yarn.

Give an old frame a new look with glue and yarn. Remove the backing and glass, if any, from the frame. Working with one section at a time, paint glue on the front and back of the frame. Then wrap yarn around the frame. You may wish to change yarn colors as you glue and wrap.

Compact Disk Case Picture Frames

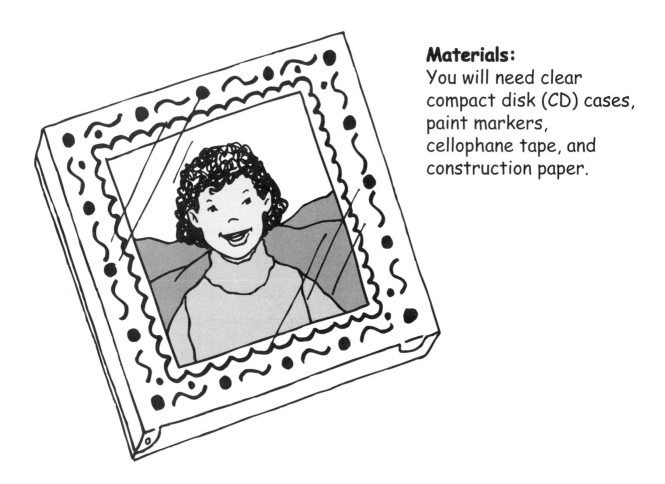

Materials:
You will need clear compact disk (CD) cases, paint markers, cellophane tape, and construction paper.

Make decorative picture frame gifts from discarded CD cases. Measure, cut, and insert a sheet of construction paper in a CD case. Use paint markers to decorate a border on each side of the case. Cut and tape a picture to the construction paper liner.

Note: Decorate both sides of the CD case and tape a picture to each side of the construction paper liner to make a double-sided frame.

Cutoff Blue Jeans Tote Bag

Materials:
You will need a pair of cutoff blue jeans, scissors, a needle and heavy thread, yarn, and fabric markers.

A

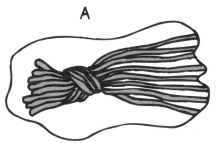

Don't throw away those jeans. Cut the legs off to make shorts, then sew them into a tote bag. Measure and cut eight equal lengths of yarn to form a strap for your tote bag. Gather the yarn and tie a knot at one end (A). Braid, then tie a knot at the end. Ask an adult to help you turn the shorts inside out and sew the leg openings closed. Turn the shorts right side out. Use paint markers to decorate your blue jean tote bag. Tie the braided yarn strap to belt loops as shown above. If there are no belt loops, ask your adult helper to sew the strap to the waistband.

Blue Jean Books

Materials:
You will need old blue jeans, scissors, a hole punch, yarn, masking tape, and fabric markers.

Make a flexible book for small children from old blue jeans and paint markers. Measure and cut several same size book pages from old blue jeans. Attach masking tape to the edges of each page. This will keep the edges from fraying. Punch holes along one side of each page. To form a book, lace and tie yarn bows through each of the holes. Use fabric markers to draw pictures of a popular children's story on each page. Then write the title and draw a picture on the cover.

Newspaper Gift Wrap

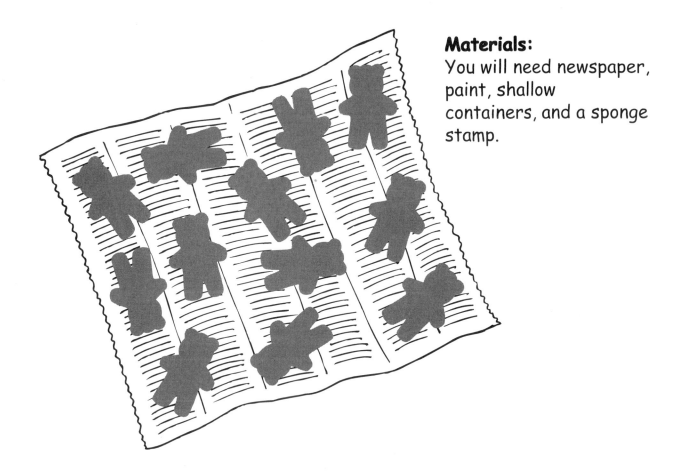

Materials:
You will need newspaper, paint, shallow containers, and a sponge stamp.

Design your own gift wrap. Draw an outline pattern to make a stamp from a sponge. Prepare your worktable with shallow containers filled with paint and sheets of newspaper. Dip the sponge stamp in the paint. Scrape excess paint along the edge of the container, then press the stamp on a sheet of newspaper. Continue stamping the sheet of newspaper until you create the design or pattern you want.

Mitten Sachet

Materials:
You will need a clean old mitten, potpourri mix, ribbon, scissors, construction paper, markers, and a hole punch.

Make a mitten sachet to give to a friend or relative. Fill an old mitten with store-bought potpourri mix. Copy, color, cut out, and punch a hole in a construction paper gift tag (below). Cut and thread a length of ribbon through the hole in the tag, then tie the ribbon into a bow around the wrist of the mitten.

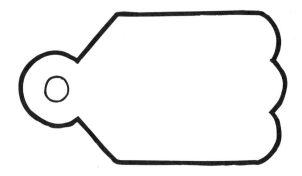

Paint Can Game Tote

Materials:
You will need a large, clean paint can, construction paper, scissors, glue, and markers.

Transform an empty paint can into a traveling tote for small games such as a tic-tac-toe board and playing pieces, jacks, marbles, chalk for a game of hopscotch, and a note pad and pen to play a game of connect-the-dots. Measure, decorate, cut, and glue a sheet of construction paper around the paint can. Place small games and playing pieces in the can.

Egg Carton Jewelry Box

Materials:
You will need a clean Styrofoam egg carton, markers, glitter, ribbon, buttons, pasta noodles, yarn, scissors, and glue.

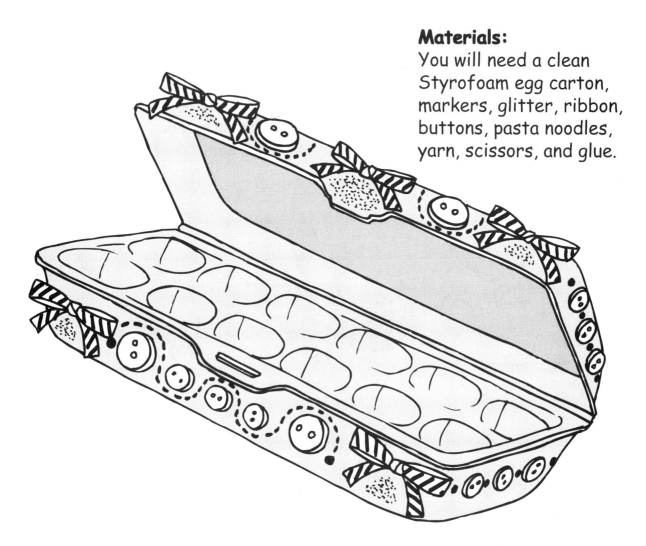

Make a handy jewelry box with 12 separate compartments from a Styrofoam egg carton. Decorate the outside of the carton with one or more of the craft supplies listed above. Use markers to add additional decorative details.

How to Make Crafts from Trash ©2002 Monday Morning Books, Inc.

Poster Board Memory Quilt

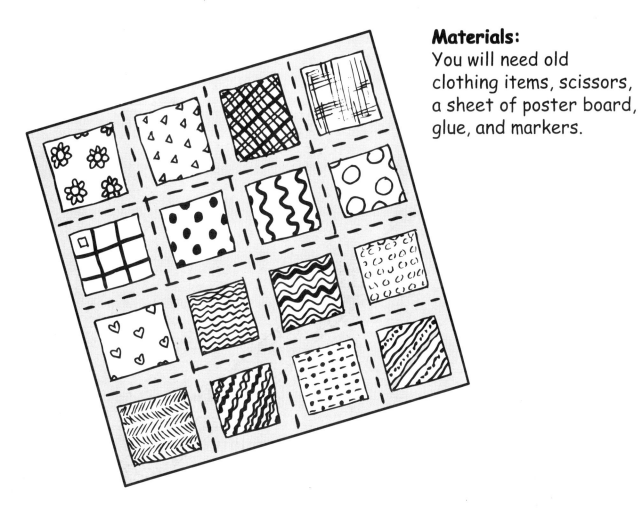

Materials:
You will need old clothing items, scissors, a sheet of poster board, glue, and markers.

Create a poster board memory quilt for display from clothing items that no longer fit or are damaged. Measure and cut a sheet of poster board into a square. Then measure and draw stitch lines to form a 16 square grid on the poster board. Cut squares from clothing items smaller than the poster board squares . Glue a cloth square in the center of each square on the grid.

Painted Walking Stick

Materials:
You will need an old broomstick, yarn, glue, and paint markers.

Make a colorful walking stick from an old broomstick. Use paint markers to decorate the broomstick, then wrap and glue yarn around the stick. Give the walking stick to a friend or family member to use on hikes in the park or the woods. The walking stick can also be hung on a wall.

Plastic Milk Bottle Bookmarks

Materials:
You will need a large plastic milk bottle, scissors, a hole punch, ribbon or yarn, and paint markers.

Make plastic bookmarks for your friends and relatives from a clean plastic milk bottle. Cut rectangle bookmarks from the sides of a milk bottle (A). Use paint markers to decorate each bookmark. Then punch a hole and tie a length of ribbon or yarn to each bookmark.

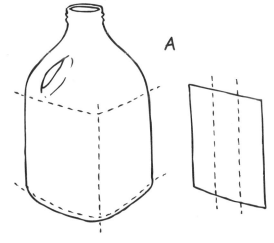

A

Ribbon Clad Flower Pot

Materials:
You will need an old flower pot, assorted ribbon, scissors, and glue.

Make an attractive storage container for hair brushes, pens and pencils, or utensils from an old flower pot. Cut and glue assorted ribbon around the outside of a clean clay or plastic flower pot. Then cut, tie, and glue a large ribbon bow to the rim.

Canada Day
Canada Day Flower Pot

Materials:
You will need a clay flower pot and dish, a red paint marker, and a plastic lid maple leaf template.

Decorate an old clay flower pot with red maple leaves for Canada Day. Copy the pattern below to make a plastic lid template. Use the template to trace maple leaves around the pot. Then color the leaves with a red paint marker.

Canada Day
Maple Leaf Sponge Stencilling

Materials:
You will need a brown grocery bag, a paint stirrer, a sponge, scissors, a shallow container, a stapler, yarn, and red paint.

Create a maple leaf stencilled painting to display on Canada Day. Cut one side from a brown grocery bag. Make a maple leaf sponge stamp. Prepare a worktable covered with newspaper, and a shallow container filled with red paint. Dip the leaf stencil in the paint. Scrape excess paint along the edge of the container, then press the leaf on your grocery bag sheet. Continue stencilling until you create the design or pattern you want. When the paint has dried, staple the top edge of your painting to a paint stirrer. Cut and staple a length of yarn to each end of the stirrer for hanging.

Chinese New Year
Egg Carton Dragons

Materials:
You will need a Styrofoam egg carton, green and yellow construction paper, markers, scissors, glitter, and glue.

Make a pair of yellow, blue, pink, or green Chinese New Year dragons from Styrofoam egg cartons. Cut the top off of an egg carton, then cut the egg cups apart lengthwise, into two six cup sections. Use markers to draw faces and scales on the cups. Cut and glue yellow and green triangles to the egg cups. Add sparkle to your dragon with glue and glitter.

Chinese New Year
Plastic Lid Animal Coasters

Materials:
You will need 12 plastic margarine tub lids and paint markers.

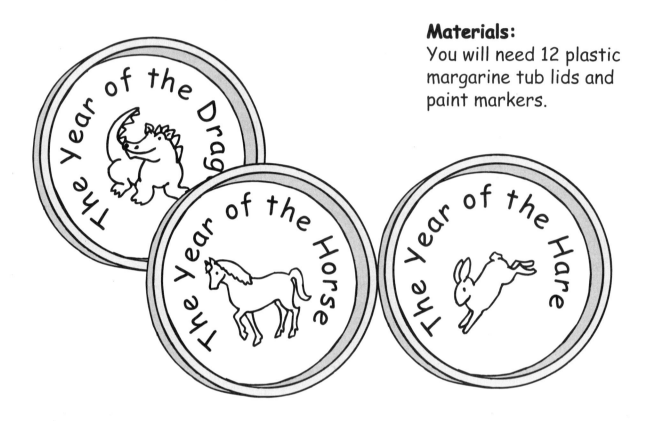

Make festive Chinese New Year coasters from margarine tub lids. Use paint markers to draw each of the animal patterns below on the inside of a plastic lid or draw your own.

Christmas

Styrofoam Tray Christmas Tree

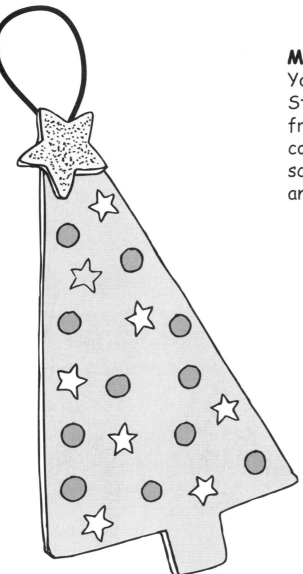

Materials:

You will need a clean Styrofoam vegetable or fruit tray, markers, construction paper, scissors, yarn glitter, and glue.

Make a tree ornament from Styrofoam trays. Draw a tree as shown above on a Styrofoam tray. Ask an adult to use a craft knife to cut out the tree. Draw and cut out a star for the top of your tree from the scrap pieces. Apply glue and glitter to the star then glue it on the tree. Decorate your tree with construction paper ornaments. Cut and glue a yarn hanger to the back of the tree.

Christmas
Old Compact Disk Tree Ornaments

Materials:
You will need discarded compact disks (CDs), permanent or paint markers, ribbon, construction paper, scissors, and glue.

Make tree ornaments from discarded or damaged compact disks (CDs). To decorate your CDs: Use paint or permanent markers to draw a repeating pattern around the disk. Cut out and glue small construction paper shapes to both sides of a disk. Write the first words from a holiday song on each side of a disk. Cut and tie a ribbon loop through the center of the disk, then tie a ribbon bow around the loop as shown above.

Christmas
Plastic Snowman Bookmarks

Materials:
You will need a plastic milk container, scissors, and paint markers.

A

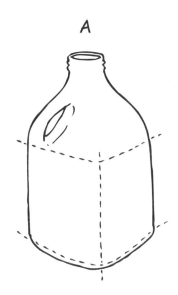

Make bookmarks from plastic milk containers. Cut out the sides from a plastic milk container (A). Copy the snowman shape below onto the plastic sheets and cut out. Use paint markers to decorate the bookmarks.

Cinco de Mayo

Cinco de Mayo Display Plate

Materials:
You will need a discarded plate, permanent markers, white construction paper, glue, and ribbon.

Make a festive plate decoration for Cinco de Mayo from a discarded plate. Copy and cut out the medallion shown here or create a design of your own. Use green and red markers to color the medallion. Glue the medallion to the center of your plate. Use permanent markers to decorate the rim of the plate. Then cut, tie, and glue a red, green, and white ribbon bow to the top of your plate.

114

Cinco de Mayo
Styrofoam Tray Lacing Cards

Materials:
You will need a white Styrofoam vegetable or fruit tray, a hole punch, red and green markers, cellophane tape, and red yarn.

Make a Cinco de Mayo Styrofoam plaque. Punch holes around the edge of a clean, white Styrofoam tray. Lace red yarn through the holes and tape the ends to the back of the tray. Then use a red and green marker to write "Celebrate Cinco de Mayo" in the center of the tray.

Diwali

Glass Jar Dipa Lamps

Materials:
You will need a clean baby food jar, paint markers, an empty thread spool, a pipe cleaner, yellow construction paper, scissors, and cellophane tape.

Make a dipa lamp to display during Diwali from a clean baby food jar. Decorate the outside of the jar with paint markers. Copy, cut out, and tape a yellow construction paper flame to a pipe cleaner length. Then place it in the spool hole. Place the candle in your glass jar dipa lamp.

Diwali

Aluminum Pie Tin Dipa Lamps

Materials:
You will need a small aluminum pie tin, permanent markers, an empty thread spool, a pipe cleaner, yellow construction paper, scissors, and cellophane tape.

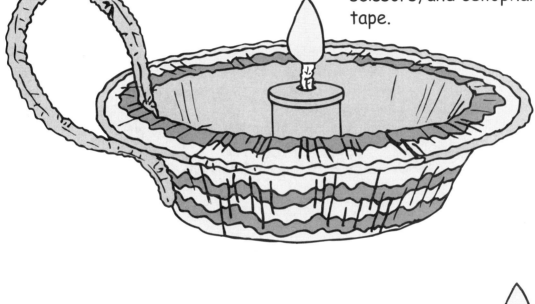

Make a dipa lamp from a small aluminum pie tin. Decorate a pie tin with permanent markers. Bend and staple a pipe cleaner handle to the pie tin as shown above. Copy, cut out, and tape a yellow construction paper flame to a pipe cleaner length. Then place it in the spool hole. Place the candle in the pie tin. Display your aluminum dipa lamp during Diwali.

Easter
Sawdust and Glue Egg Basket

Materials:
You will need an old bowl, newspaper, glue, sawdust, and a mixing container.

Make a textured basket to display your Easter eggs. Glue three layers of newspaper strips to the outside of an old bowl. Combine glue and sawdust in a mixing container. Apply the sawdust mixture to the outside of the papiér mâché bowl. When the mixture has dried, carefully pry the bowl out of the sawdust form. Place decorated eggs in your sawdust basket.

Easter
Plastic Milk Bottle Bunny

Materials:
You will need a plastic milk container, scissors, and paint markers.

A

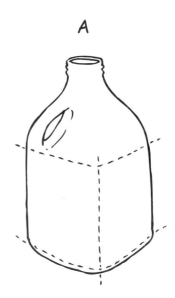

Make bookmarks from plastic milk containers. Cut out the sides from a plastic milk container (A). Copy the rabbit shape below onto the plastic sheets and cut out. Use paint markers to decorate the bookmarks.

Easter
Grocery Bag Bunny Basket

Materials:
You will need a brown grocery bag, scissors, pink construction paper, markers, pipe cleaners, and glue.

Make a bunny basket from a brown grocery bag. Draw bunny ears on one side of a brown grocery bag. Cut out the ears and the back of the bag as shown above. Cut out and glue pink ear liners as shown. Use a marker to draw features and cut and glue pipe cleaner whiskers on your grocery bag bunny's face.

Easter
Woven Berry Basket

Materials:
You will need a berry basket, a large button, cellophane tape, and yarn.

Make a basket for small candy eggs from a berry basket. Tie a large button to the end of a length of yarn. Lace the yarn, from the inside out, through a hole at the bottom of a berry basket. Weave the yarn through the holes. Tie additional lengths of yarn as you continue weaving. Cut and tape the end of the yarn to the inside of the basket. Fill your basket with candy eggs.

Easter
Jelly Bean Dispenser

Materials:
You will need a clean dry juice jar, paint markers, and jelly beans.

Make a jelly bean dispenser from a juice jar. Use paint markers to decorate the lid and outside of a clean dry juice jar. Fill the jar with jelly beans.

Father's Day
Paper Towel Tube Tie Rack

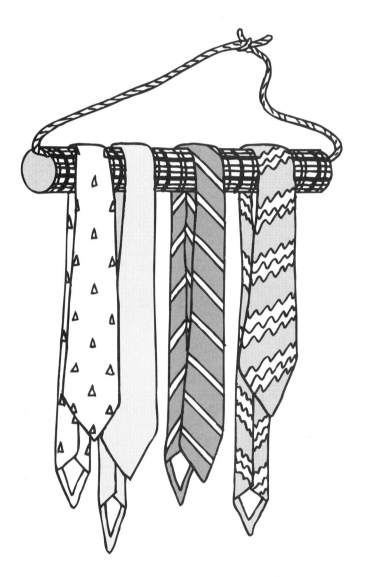

Materials:
You will need a paper towel tube, gift wrap or wallpaper scraps, scissors, glue, and yarn.

Make a tie rack for a Father's Day gift from a paper towel tube. Measure, cut, and glue gift wrap or wallpaper around a paper towel tube. Cut, thread, and tie a length of yarn through the tube.

Father's Day
Plastic Lid Sock Matchers

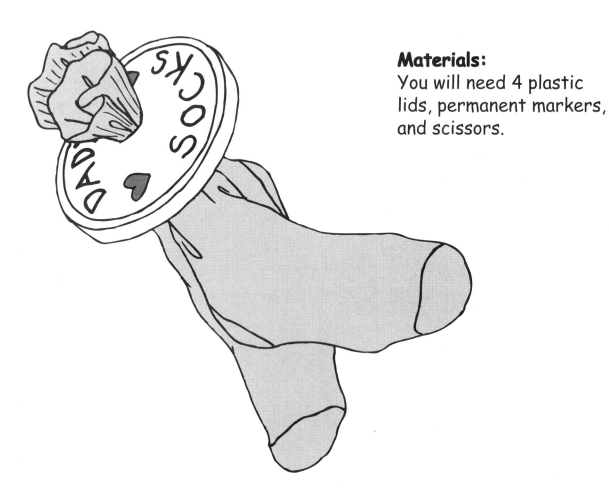

Materials:
You will need 4 plastic lids, permanent markers, and scissors.

Make plastic lid sock matchers for a Father's Day gift. Use paint markers to decorate and write "Dad's Socks" on each side of the lids. Cut a hole in the center of each lid as shown (A). Show Dad how to push the open end of a matching pair of socks through the hole in each lid.

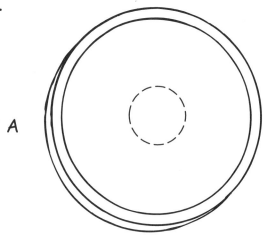

A

How to Make Crafts from Trash ©2002 Monday Morning Books, Inc.

Hanukkah
Dinner Plate Menorah

Materials:
You will need an old dinner plate, construction paper, scissors, glue, and paint markers.

Make a dinner plate menorah to display during Hanukkah. Measure and cut a construction paper half circle to fit in the center of an old dinner plate. Draw eight lines on the half circle as shown below (A). Color and glue the half circle to the plate. Copy, color, cut out, and glue nine candles as shown above. Then use paint markers to decorate the rim of the plate.

A

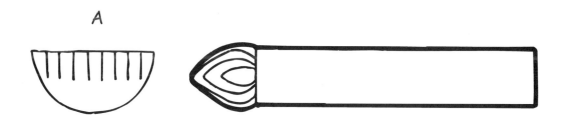

Hanukkah
Paper Cup Menorah

Materials:
You will need nine small paper cups, buttons, markers, yellow craft tissue, glue, and a sheet of corrugated board.

Make a menorah from paper cups. Use markers to decorate the outside of each cup. Glue buttons around each cup. Cut a slit in the bottom of each cup and insert a yellow craft tissue flame. Measure, cut, and glue construction paper to a long narrow sheet of corrugated cardboard. Glue each candle to the cardboard, then write "Happy Hanukkah" on the cardboard.

Hanukkah
Plastic Lid Menorah Display

Materials:
You will need paper towel tubes, small plastic lids, paint markers, scissors, glue, construction paper, and a sheet of corrugated cardboard.

Make a menorah from paper towel tubes and small plastic lids. Measure, cut, and color nine equal size paper towel tube candles. Draw a flame in the center of nine small plastic lids. Cut two slits at the bottom of each lid as shown here. Then slide a lid onto each candle. Measure, cut, and glue construction paper to a long narrow sheet of corrugated cardboard. Glue each candle to the cardboard, then write "Happy Hanukkah" on the cardboard.

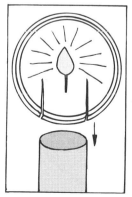

Halloween
Styrofoam Tray Pumpkin Garlands

Materials:
You will need clean
Styrofoam trays,
scissors, markers, a hole
punch, and yarn.

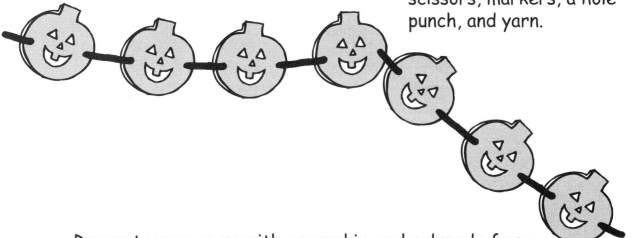

Decorate your room with a pumpkin garland made from
Styrofoam trays. Copy and cut out pumpkin shapes (below) from
Styrofoam trays. Use markers to color and add features to each
pumpkin. Then punch two holes and lace yarn through each pumpkin.

Halloween
Milk Container Jack-o'-lantern

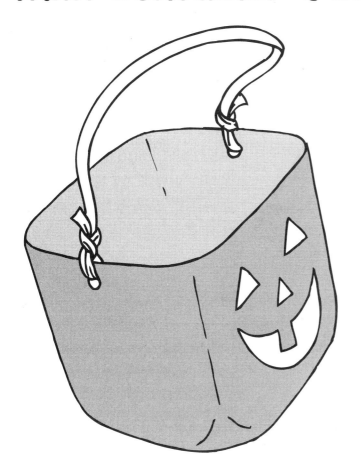

Materials:
You will need a large clean plastic milk container, scissors, paint markers, a hole punch, and ribbon.

Make a jack-o'-lantern to carry your treats from a plastic milk container. Cut the top off of a plastic milk container as shown below. Use paint markers to color and add features to the container. Punch two holes, then lace and tie a ribbon handle through each hole to make a jack-o'-lantern.

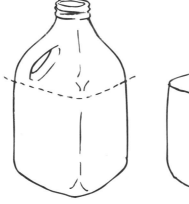

Halloween
Jar Lid Pumpkin Checkers

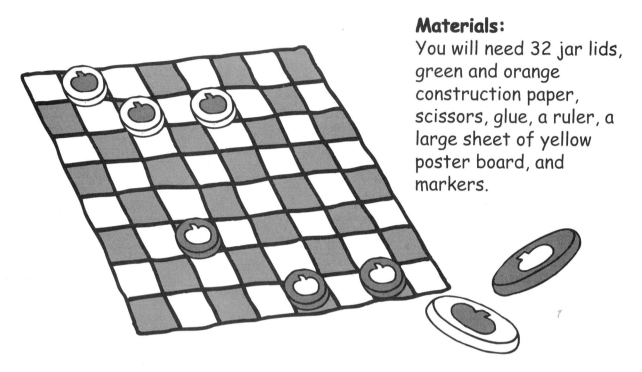

Materials:
You will need 32 jar lids, green and orange construction paper, scissors, glue, a ruler, a large sheet of yellow poster board, and markers.

Make pumpkin checkers from jar lids. Copy and cut out 16 orange and 16 green pumpkins (below). Glue a pumpkin to the top of each jar lid. Measure and cut a large sheet of yellow poster board into a square. Then use a ruler to measure 8 equal columns in each direction as shown above. Color every other block on the board, purple. Set up your board and ask a friend to play.

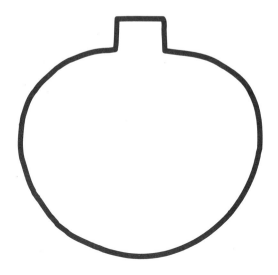

Independence Day
Stars and Stripes Sleeve Hats

Materials:
You will need an old white long-sleeved knit shirt, scissors, fabric markers, and yarn.

Make hats to wear on Independence Day from knit shirt sleeves. Cut the sleeves from an old long-sleeved knit shirt. Use fabric markers to draw stars and stripes designs on each sleeve. Fold over the shoulder edge of each sleeve to finish your design. Then cut and tie a length of yarn around the cuff of each sleeve.

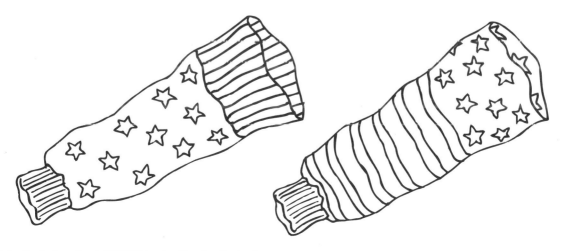

Independence Day
Stars and Stripes Lid Badges

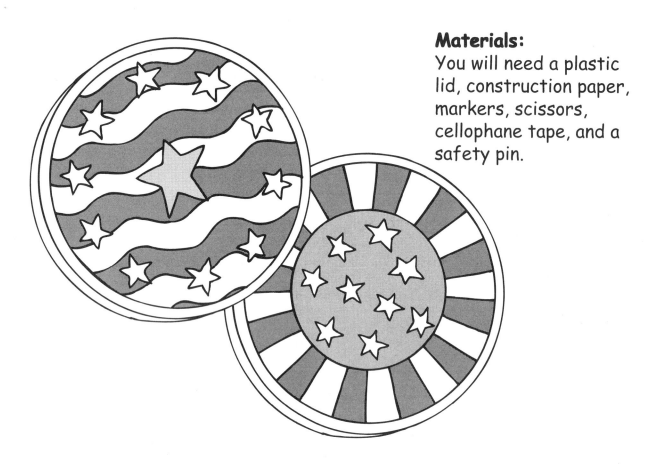

Materials:
You will need a plastic lid, construction paper, markers, scissors, cellophane tape, and a safety pin.

Make a badge to wear on Independence Day from a plastic lid. Measure and cut out a construction paper circle to fit in the center of a plastic lid. Copy the designs shown above onto the construction paper circle or create one of your own. Attach a tape loop, sticky side out, to the back of the construction paper circle. Then attach it to the lid. Tape a safety pin to the back of the lid as shown here to form a badge.

Back of badge

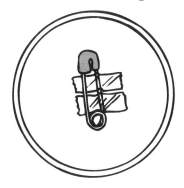

Kwanzaa
Egg Carton Kinara

Materials:
You will need a Styrofoam egg carton, scissors, red, green, and black markers, 7 craft sticks, yellow construction paper, glue, and a sheet of corrugated board.

Make a kinara to display during Kwanzaa from egg carton cups. Cut seven cups from a Styrofoam egg carton. Decorate three cups with a red marker, three cups with a green marker, and the last cup with a black marker. Copy and cut out seven yellow construction paper flames (below) and glue one to each of seven craft sticks. Cut a slit and insert a craft stick candle in the bottom of each cup. Measure, cut, and glue construction paper to a long narrow sheet of corrugated cardboard. Glue each candle to the cardboard, then write "Happy Kwanzaa" on the cardboard.

Kwanzaa
Old Baseball Cap Holiday Hat

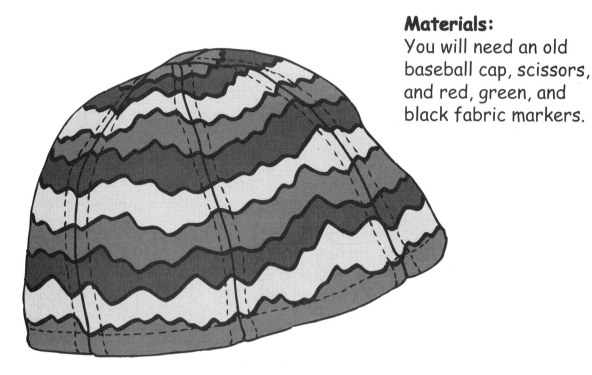

Materials:
You will need an old baseball cap, scissors, and red, green, and black fabric markers.

Make a hat to wear during the celebration of Kwanzaa from an old baseball cap. Cut the bill off a baseball cap as shown below. Use red, green, and black fabric markers to decorate the cutoff cap as shown above or create a design of your own.

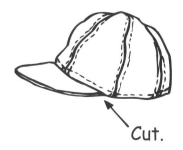

Cut.

How to Make Crafts from Trash ©2002 Monday Morning Books, Inc.

Mardi Gras
Mardi Gras Button Necklaces

Materials:
You will need yarn, a twist tie needle, and assorted buttons.

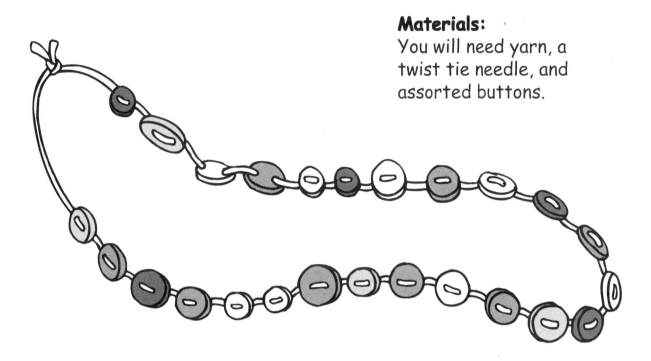

Make button necklaces to wear during Mardi Gras. Measure and cut several lengths of yarn. Use a twist tie needle to thread yarn through button holes, then tie the loose yarn ends together.

Note: If you are unable to collect enough buttons to make several necklaces, substitute real buttons with poster board buttons. Copy, color, and cut out poster board buttons (below), or create a button designs of your own.

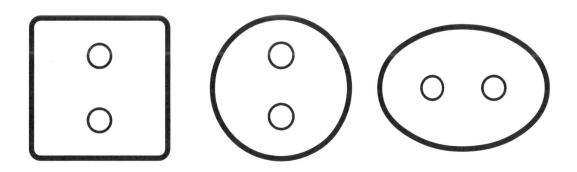

Mardi Gras
Paper Bead Necklaces

Materials:
You will need gift wrap scraps or color magazine pictures, scissors, glue, a twist tie needle, and yarn.

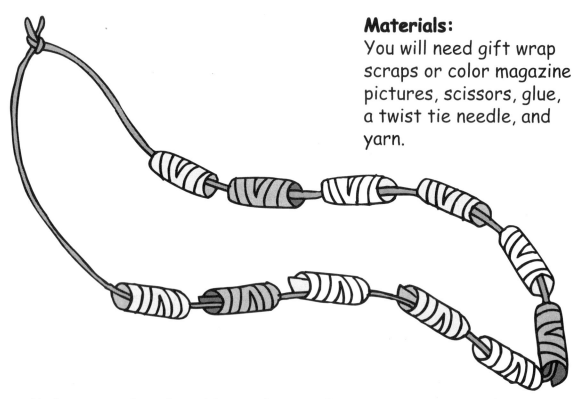

Make paper bead necklaces from gift wrap scraps or color magazine pictures. Cut gift wrap or magazine picture triangles (below). Apply glue (A), then form a bead by rolling the wide end of the triangle towards the narrow end (B). When the glue has dried, use a twist tie needle to thread yarn through the beads. Then tie the loose yarn ends together.

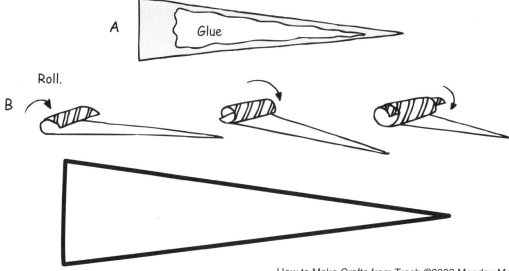

How to Make Crafts from Trash ©2002 Monday Morning Books, Inc.

Mardi Gras
Tray and Egg Carton Masks

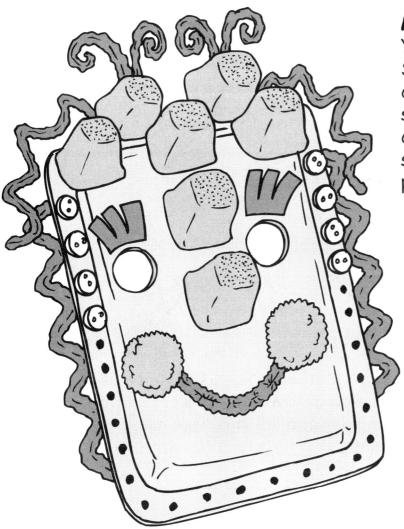

Materials:
You will need a clean Styrofoam tray and egg carton, markers, scissors, glitter, pipe cleaners, buttons, stickers, construction paper, and pompoms.

Make a Mardi Gras mask from a Styrofoam tray and egg carton. Cut the cups from a Styrofoam egg carton. Then cut two eye holes in a Styrofoam tray. Use markers, construction paper, pipe cleaners, buttons, pompoms, glue, and glitter to decorate your mask.

Mother's Day
Mom's Keys Margarine Lid

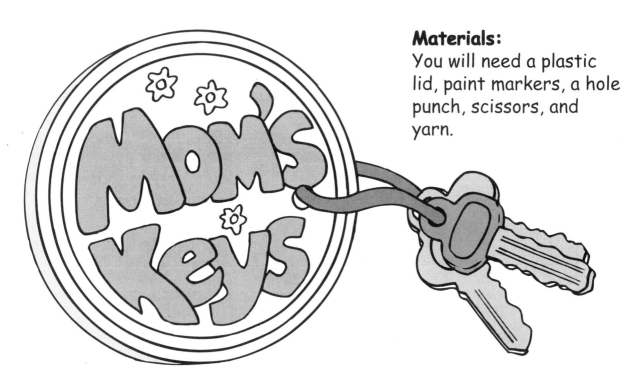

Materials:
You will need a plastic lid, paint markers, a hole punch, scissors, and yarn.

Make a plastic key ring for a Mother's Day gift. Use paint markers to copy the design below onto a plastic lid or create a design of your own. Punch a hole in the lid, then lace and tie a length of yarn through the hole.

How to Make Crafts from Trash ©2002 Monday Morning Books, Inc.

Mother's Day
Greeting Card Flower Bouquet

Materials:
You will need old greeting cards, scissors, pipe cleaners, a stapler, and ribbon.

Make a bouquet of greeting card flower cutouts for a Mother's Day gift. Use the patterns below to copy and cut out flower shapes from greeting cards. Staple a pipe cleaner stem to the back of each flower shape. Cut and tie a ribbon bow around the stems.

Mother's Day
Flower Wreath

Materials:
You will need a paper plate, scissors, discarded artificial flowers, pipe cleaners, ribbon, glue, and a stapler.

Make a flower wreath for Mother's Day from discarded artificial flowers. Fold and cut out a circle from the center of a paper plate (A and B). Cut the stems from discarded artificial flowers. Twist, bend, and glue pipe cleaners around the paper plate wreath form. Then glue artificial flowers and bows around the paper plate wreath. Cut and staple a ribbon hanger to the top of your artificial flower wreath.

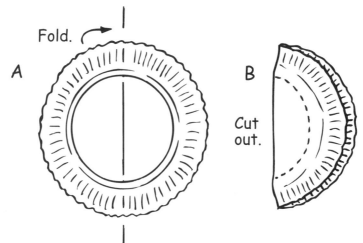

Fold.

A

B

Cut out.

St. Patrick's Day
ShamRocks

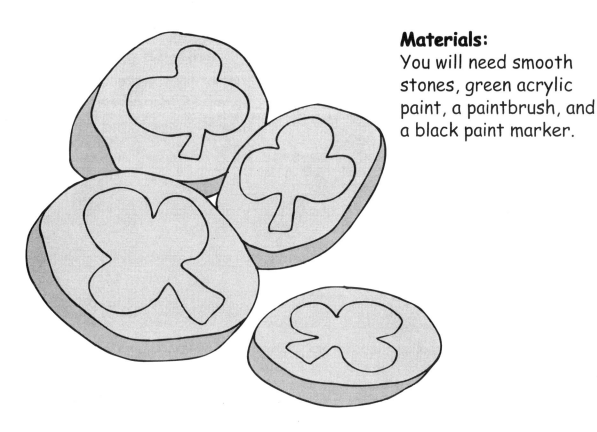

Materials:
You will need smooth stones, green acrylic paint, a paintbrush, and a black paint marker.

Make ShamRocks to give to your friends and relatives on St. Patrick's Day. Paint each stone green. When the green paint has dried, use a black paint marker to copy the shamrock pattern below onto each stone.

St. Patrick's Day
Paper Cup Leprechauns

Materials:
You will need paper cups, markers, construction paper, scissors, glue, pipe cleaners, and small pompoms.

Make leprechauns to display on St. Patrick's Day. Color the top and bottom portions of each paper cup green. Copy, cut out, and color two each of the construction paper collar and shoe patterns, a shamrock, and a bow tie. Glue the patterns, a pipe cleaner hat brim, and small pompom buttons to the cup as shown above. Then draw a face on your leprechaun.

Bow tie: Cut one.   Collar: Cut two.   Shoe: Cut two.   Shamrock: Cut one.

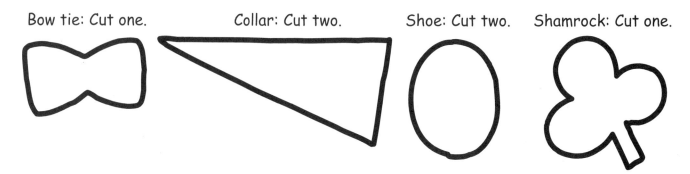

How to Make Crafts from Trash ©2002 Monday Morning Books, Inc.

St. Patrick's Day
Bottle Cap Gold Coins

Materials:
You will need bottle caps, a paintbrush, glue, gold glitter, and a bowl.

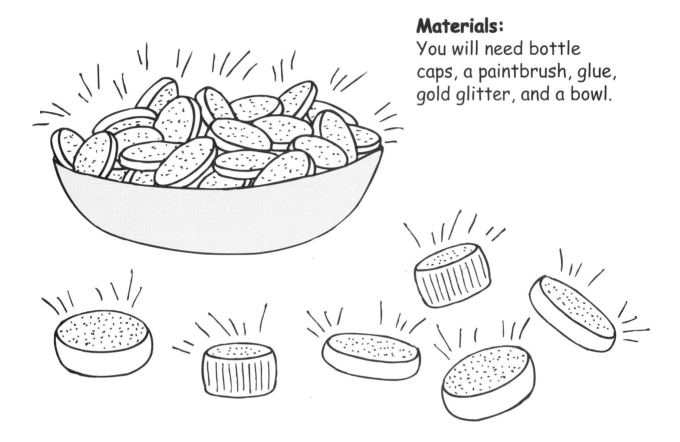

Fill a bowl with glittery gold coins made from discarded bottle caps to give away on St. Patrick's Day. Use a paintbrush to apply glue to the tops of bottle caps. Then sprinkle the caps with gold glitter. When the glue has dried, place the bottle cap gold coins in a bowl.

Thanksgiving
Grocery Bag Cornucopia Collage

Materials:
You will need a brown grocery bag, scissors, a stapler, poster board, construction paper, markers, and glue

A

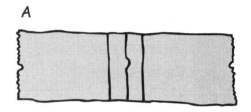

B

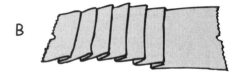

C

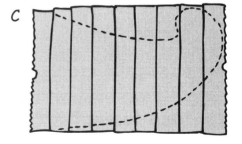

Make a unique cornucopia collage from a brown grocery bag. Cut out the sides of a brown grocery bag (A). Accordion fold the grocery bag sheet, forming pockets, as shown (B). Draw and cut out a cornucopia shape from the folded grocery bag. Staple the outer edges of each fold, then glue the cornucopia to a sheet of poster board. Copy, color, and cut out construction paper fruits, vegetables, and leaves. Place the cutouts in the cornucopia pockets.

144

Thanksgiving
Old Baseball Cap Turkey

Materials:
You will need an old baseball cap, scissors, a permanent black marker, construction paper, a pair of wiggly eyes, one large orange pompom, glue, and fabric markers.

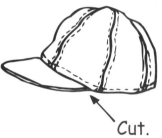

Cut.

Make a turkey decoration to display on Thanksgiving from an old baseball cap. Cut the bill off a baseball cap as shown above. Use a permanent black marker to draw feathers around the cap. Copy, cut out, and glue brown construction paper feathers to the back of the cap. Copy, cut out, fold, and glue a brown beak and a pair of wiggly eyes to a large orange pompom. Glue the pompom head to the top of the cap. Then copy, cut out, and glue a red wattle under the turkey's chin.

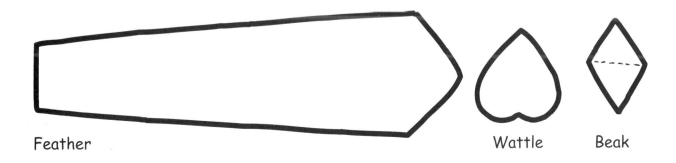

Feather   Wattle   Beak

Thanksgiving

Ten Little Turkeys Glove Puppets

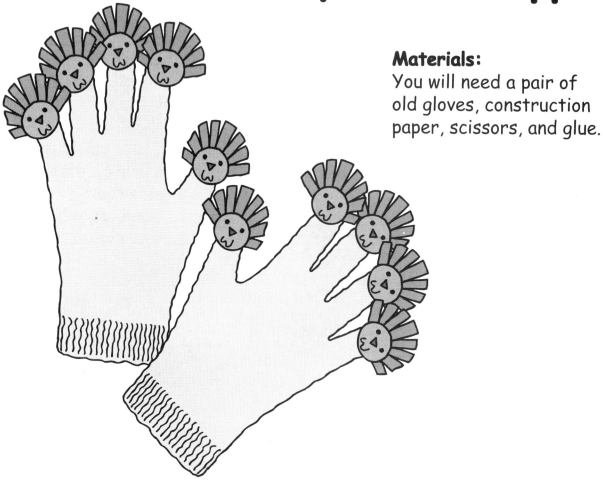

Materials:
You will need a pair of old gloves, construction paper, scissors, and glue.

Make two hands full of turkey puppets from a pair of old gloves. Copy and cut out ten feather patterns. Cut slits to divide the feathers (A). Copy and cut out ten orange heads and ten brown beaks. Fold and glue a beak to each head. Assemble and glue a head and feather pattern to each finger on each glove.

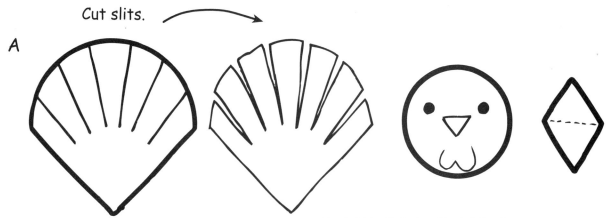

Cut slits.

A

Valentine's Day
Wallpaper Heart Pocket

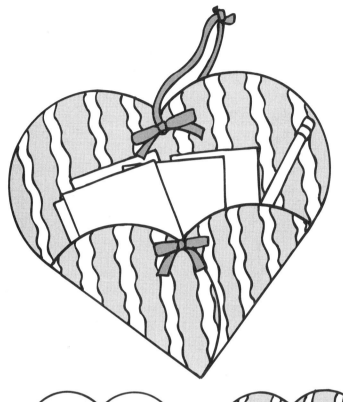

Materials:
You will need wallpaper, craft tissue, a hole punch, ribbon or yarn, scissors, a stapler, glue, note paper, a pencil or pen, and individually wrapped candy.

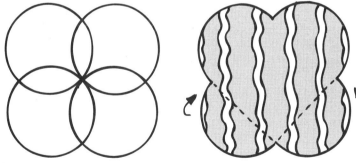 

Glue two sheets of wallpaper, back to back. Use a small plate to draw four circles on a sheet of wallpaper as shown above. Cut out the pattern, then fold over and staple two flaps to form a heart pocket. Cut, tie, and glue a ribbon bow to cover the staple. Punch a hole at the top of the heart. Lace and tie a yarn hanger through the hole, then glue a ribbon bow over the hole. Place note paper and a pencil or pen inside the pocket. Use a pushpin to hang your pocket on a display board.

Stuffed Grocery Bag Heart

For
My
Valentine

Materials:
You will need a brown grocery bag, scissors, a stapler, newspaper, and yarn.

Make a Valentine for a friend or relative from a grocery bag. Cut two large hearts from a brown grocery bag. Staple the hearts together along the top and sides leaving the bottom open. Tear and stuff strips of newspaper inside the grocery bag heart, then staple the bottom edge closed. Cut and glue a yarn bow and write a message on the heart.

Buttons and Bottle Caps Mobile

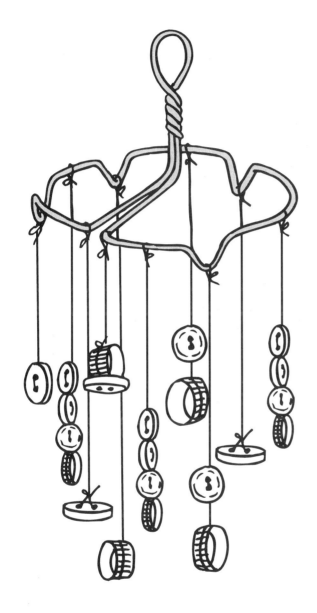

Materials:
You will need a wire hanger, pliers, buttons, bottle caps, scissors, glue, and heavy thread.

Make a mobile with bottle caps and buttons. Ask an adult to use pliers to bend a hanger for your mobile (A through C). Cut and tie heavy thread around the outer edge of bottle caps and through button holes. Then tie each loose end of thread around your wire mobile hanger.

A

B   C

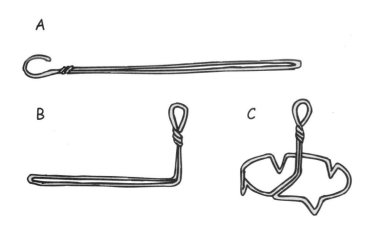

Gift Bows Mobile

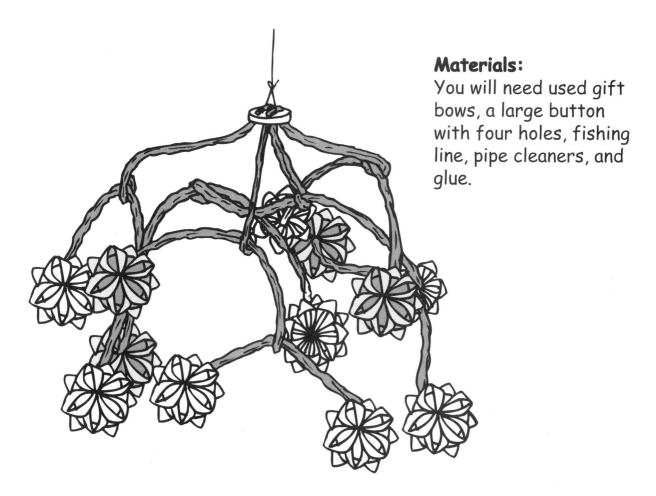

Materials:
You will need used gift bows, a large button with four holes, fishing line, pipe cleaners, and glue.

Make a mobile with gift bows and pipe cleaners. Lace and tie a length of fishing line through the holes in a large button. Then thread a pipe cleaner through each pair of holes. Form piggyback stems by bending a loop at the end of a pipe cleaner and wrapping the loop around another pipe cleaner. Glue gift bows to the ends of pipe cleaner stems. For longer mobiles, add more piggyback stems.

Greeting Card Mobile

Materials:
You will need a wire hanger, pliers, old greeting cards, a hole punch, scissors, and heavy thread.

Make a mobile with old greeting cards. Ask an adult to use pliers to bend a hanger for your mobile (A through C). Punch a hole and tie a length of heavy thread at the top of each greeting card. Tie each loose end of thread around the wire mobile hanger. To form piggyback levels, punch two additional holes at the bottom of each card, then tie on more cards.

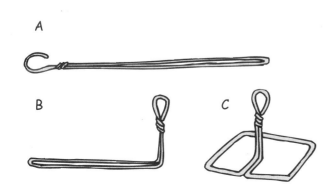

A

B   C

Styrofoam Fish Mobile

Materials:
You will need Styrofoam trays, markers, a wire hanger, construction paper, a stapler, scissors, glue, and heavy thread.

Make a mobile with cutout Styrofoam fish. Measure and cut two ocean waves from a sheet of construction paper. Sandwich and staple a wire hanger between the wave patterns. Copy, color, and cut out fish from Styrofoam trays. Measure and cut different lengths of heavy thread and staple one to each of your fish. Then tie the loose ends of thread around the wire hanger.

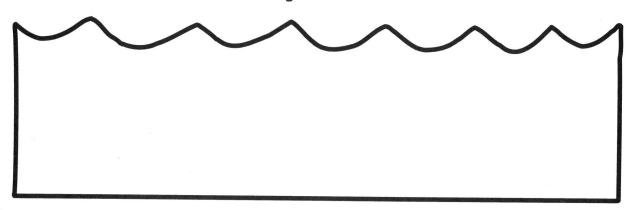

Paper Towel Roll Mobile

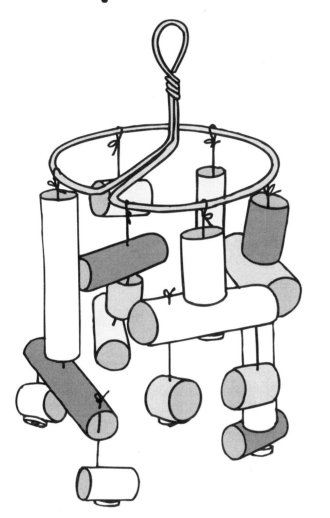

Materials:
You will need a wire hanger, pliers, paper towel tubes, markers, buttons, scissors, a twist tie needle, and heavy thread.

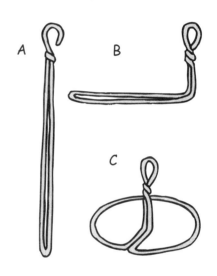

Make a mobile from paper towel tubes. Ask an adult to use pliers to bend a hanger for your mobile (A through C). Cut and color paper towel tubes with markers. Start each tube strand by tying a button to one end of a length of heavy thread. Then pierce two holes and use a twist tie needle to lace the thread through a horizontal tube (D). Add another vertical or horizontal tube (E), then tie the loose end of thread around your wire mobile hanger. To form piggyback levels, punch a set of holes at both ends of a horizontal tube, then tie on more tube strands.

Jewelry Shoe Box

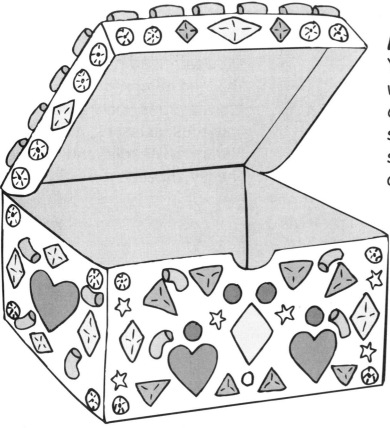

Materials:
You will need a shoe box with a hinged lid, construction paper, glue, scissors, sequins, stickers, pasta noodles, and markers.

Turn a shoe box into an attractive storage box. Measure, cut, and glue construction paper to the inside and outside of a shoe box and lid. Decorate the outside of the shoe box with cutout jewel shapes (below), sequins, stickers, and pasta noodles. Use markers to add decorative details.

Note: If you do not have a hinged lid shoe box, cut a slit in two corners of the lid. Then attach the lid to the box with a strip of wide masking tape before decorating.

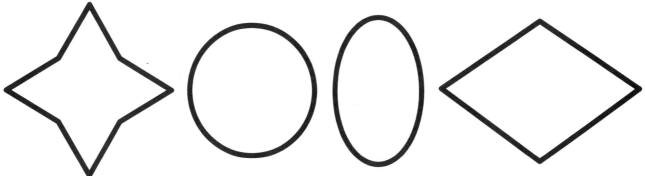

File Box Treasure Chest

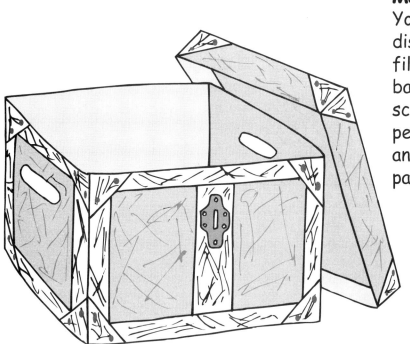

Materials:
You will need a discarded cardboard file box, brown grocery bags, aluminum foil, scissors, glue, a permanent black marker, and yellow construction paper.

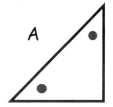

Make a treasure chest from a discarded cardboard file box. Crumple, then flatten and cut sheets from grocery bags. Glue to the outside of the file box. Tear and glue sheets of aluminum foil along the edges and down the center of the front and back of the box and lid. Then form 24 aluminum foil triangles and glue each to a corner of the file box and lid. Draw nail heads on the triangles with a permanent black marker (A). Then cut out and glue a yellow construction paper lock to the front of your treasure chest.

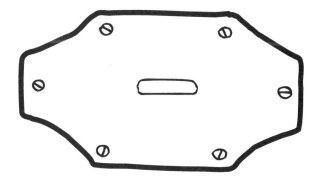

Textured Coffee Cans

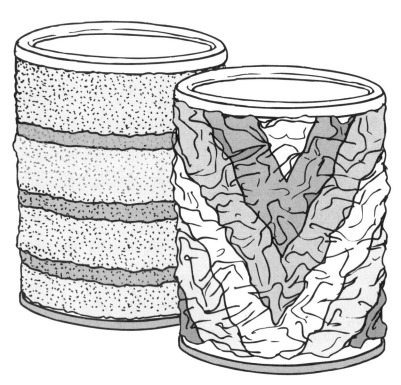

Materials:
You will need large empty coffee cans with lids, mixing containers, paintbrush, acrylic paint, sand, glue, and cloth scraps.

Transform coffee cans into textured storage containers.

Sandy Paint: Mix acrylic paint and sand in a container. Paint the outside of a coffee can with the sandy paint. Mix additional colors in separate containers.

Wrinkled Cloth: Cut and dip cloth scraps in glue to cover the outside of a coffee can. Pinch the cloth to form wrinkles. When the glue has dried, use acrylic paint to create a design on your wrinkled coffee can.

Bean Mosaic Cookie Can

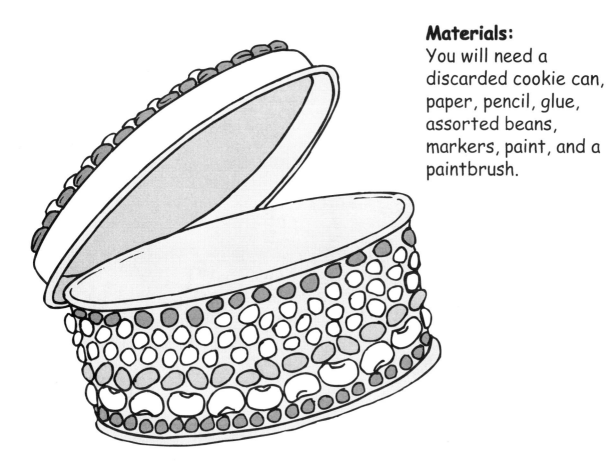

Materials:
You will need a discarded cookie can, paper, pencil, glue, assorted beans, markers, paint, and a paintbrush.

Make a bean mosaic storage container from a discarded cookie can. Before you begin, plan your design on a sheet of paper. Then glue beans to the outside of the can and lid following your design.

Optional: You can use markers or paint to add color to your bean mosaic.

Cereal Box Magazine Holders

Materials:
You will need large cereal boxes, scissors, glue, gift wrap, and construction paper.

Turn a large cereal box into a magazine storage box. Cut the front, back, and one side of a cereal box as shown above. Measure, cut, and glue gift wrap to the box. Overlap gift wrap around the cut edges. Cut and glue a construction paper label to the short side of the box. Write the name of the magazine or the type of magazines you will store in the box. Make additional boxes for more magazines.

Twine Wrapped Jars

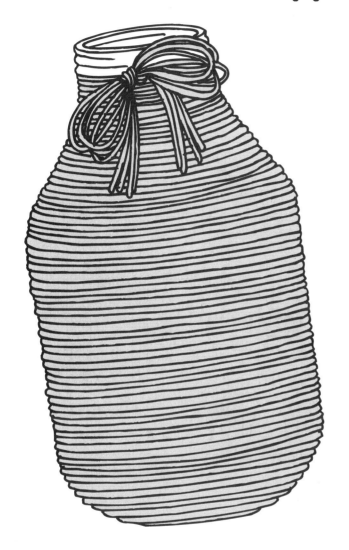

Materials:
You will need a clean glass juice jar, glue, a paintbrush, twine, markers, and paint.

Make a twine vase from a glass juice jar. Starting at the top, apply glue to a glass jar and carefully press twine into the glue as you wrap it around the jar. When the glue has dried, cut and tie several lengths of twine into a bow around the neck of your twine vase.

Optional: Use markers or paint to draw a repeating pattern or add a colorful design to your vase.

Drink Bottle Candy Dispensers

Materials:
You will need clean and dry soda bottles with lids, paint markers, and candy.

Make see-through candy dispensers from clean dry plastic soda bottles. Use paint markers to decorate the outside of a plastic soda bottle. Make sure the inside of the bottle and lid are dry, then fill it with candy. Write the name of the contents on the bottle. Make a dispenser for candy corn, jelly beans, raisins, peanuts, gum balls, wrapped candies, and more.